The Creeks

BIBLIOGRAPHICAL SERIES

The Newberry Library Center
for the History of the American Indian

General Editor
Francis Jennings
Assistant Editor
William R. Swagerty

The Center Is Supported by Grants from

The National Endowment for the Humanities
The Ford Foundation
The W. Clement and Jessie V. Stone Foundation
The Woods Charitable Fund, Inc.
Mr. Gaylord Donnelley

The Creeks

A Critical Bibliography

MICHAEL D. GREEN

Published for the Newberry Library

Indiana University Press

BLOOMINGTON AND LONDON

Manufactured in the United States of America

Library of Congress Cataloging in Publication Data

Green, Michael D   1941–
    The Creeks.

    (Bibliographical series)
    Includes index.
        1. Creek Indians—Bibliography. I. Newberry Library, Chicago. II. Title. III. Series.
    Z1210.C72G72 [E99.C9] 016.97'0004'97 79–2166
    ISBN 0–253–31776–2 pbk.   1 2 3 4 5 83 82 81 80 79

CONTENTS

PREFACE: A WORD ON DEFINITIONS

The Creek Nation was a confederacy—an alliance of separate and independent tribes that gradually became, over a long period, a single political organization. Through most of its history, however, the Confederacy was a dynamic institution, constantly changing in size as tribes, for whatever reason, entered the alliance or left it. The evidence suggests that many more groups joined than withdrew. In his *History of the American Indians* [5, p. 276], James Adair, an eighteenth-century observer, asserted that, for several reasons, including "their artful policy of inviting decayed tribes to incorporate with them," the Creeks doubled their population in three mid-eighteenth-century decades. They were the only native group Adair knew of that was not declining in numbers. This means, of course, that the definition of the Creek Nation was constantly changing. This fluctuating population base has made it virtually impossible for demographers to make sensible comparative studies of the Confederacy, and it has confounded the attempts of historians and anthropologists to generalize about the Creeks. One can be clear or correct but rarely both.

Scholars know when and how some of the most recent major population changes occurred. Many Natchez people entered the Confederacy in the 1730s after French efforts to obliterate their nation. A fairly large number of Shawnees left the Confederacy in the middle decades of the eighteenth century to regroup with their kinsmen in the Ohio River valley. The Seminoles are probably the best-known emigrants from the Confederacy. In three successive phases between 1700 and 1820, argues James W. Covington in "Migration of the Seminoles into Florida, 1700–1820" [44], various bands of Creeks permanently established themselves in Florida. William C. Sturtevant, "Creek into Seminole" [184], traces the continuation and adaptation of Creek customs in Florida among the Seminoles. Together Sturtevant and Covington, whose work is much more voluminous that I have suggested here, provide an excellent introduction for students seeking further information on the Seminoles both before and after their separation from the Confederacy.

In this bibliography I have made no effort to identify the demographic movements of the constituent tribes of the Confederacy. I have further limited its scope by omitting comment upon the vast literature that analyzes either the Indian policies of European and Euro-American governments in the Southeast or the relations, generally defined, between the Creeks and their nonnative neighbors. My rule has been, in both these fields, to include only works that deal specifically and extensively with the people and tribes of the Creek Confederacy. I have thus excluded many studies that contain information on the Creeks and have included such general accounts only when they are the sole source of knowledge, however meager, on some significant facet of Creek history. Francis Paul Prucha,

A Bibliographical Guide to the History of Indian-White Relations in the United States [165], is an excellent source for titles to supplement those I have considered here.

INTRODUCTION

One of the "Five Civilized Tribes" of the American Southeast, the Creek Nation was removed along the "Trail of Tears" to the Indian Territory (Oklahoma) in the 1830s. At the time of their removal from Georgia and Alabama, the Creeks had been in contact with Europeans for nearly three hundred years. During those three centuries, despite the impetus to change, much remained the same. Creeks continued to be primarily dependent on agriculture for subsistence. Fields of corn, beans, melons, and numerous other vegetables in many varieties surrounded their towns. The forests and rivers, teeming with animals, birds, and fish, provided meat to supplement their vegetable diet and, as trade with Europeans developed, also supplied the skins and furs that purchased cloth, metal tools, guns, powder, lead, and liquor. These goods brought many changes to Creek society, the most sweeping of which was to make the people dependent on Europeans for things they had once produced for themselves.

Economic dependence, which weakened the Creeks and made them vulnerable in their dealings with Europeans, was in some measure compensated for by the rapid growth of their political and military power and prestige. The Confederacy, established in the ancient past to keep peace among the members and to provide a united front against enemies, prospered. It grew substantially in both numbers and power after the arrival of Europeans, particularly after 1680, when contact with Europeans became more or less constant. Along with this growth came a changing conception of the role of the Confederacy; organization took on new meaning, and gradually, during the eighteenth and into the nineteenth centuries, the Creek National Council assumed a policy-making and administering function that suggested the emergence of a centralized government on a European model.

Creek power declined during the nineteenth century, but not before the Confederacy had won a reputation that scholars today continue to recognize. With a population large enough to field an army of from three thousand to six thousand warriors and strategically situated between the competing English, Spanish, and French, the Creek Confederacy played a pivotal role in the history of the Southeast. Indeed, between about 1730 and 1815, the Creek Nation dominated affairs in the region. No Euro-American government could act without considering Creek wishes. But civil war and the resultant Creek War robbed the Nation of its influence. Thus weakened, it was easy for the United States to evict the Creeks. Factionalism and the United States Civil War retarded the return of national organization, but by the end of the 1860s the Creeks were establishing a constitutional republic. During the last decades of the nineteenth century, until the United States disorganized the Creek Nation with its allotment policy, the National Council functioned effectively as an independent sociopolitical institution.

Nearly 450 years have passed since De Soto led his army into the land of the Creeks. Despite disease, war, starvation, and removal, the Creek Nation survived where many native groups did not. Individuals succumbed and tribes disappeared, but the Confederacy grew. Friendship and unity were its principles; life and strength were its fruit.

RECOMMENDED WORKS

For the Beginner

[39]   David H. Corkran, *The Creek Frontier, 1540–1783.*

[52]   Angie Debo, *The Road to Disappearance.*

[84]   Donald E. Green, *The Creek People.*

[104]   Charles M. Hudson, *The Southeastern Indians.*

[191]   John R. Swanton, "Tokulki of Tulsa."

For a Basic Library

[5]   James Adair, *The History of the American Indians.*

[21]   James C. Bonner, "William McIntosh."

[33]   John W. Caughey, *McGillivray of the Creeks.*

[39]   David H. Corkran, *The Creek Frontier, 1540–1783.*

[190]   ———, *Early History of the Creek Indians.*

[193]   ———, "Religious Beliefs and Medical Practices of the Creek Indians."

[194]   ———, "Social Organization and Social Usages of the Indians of the Creek Confederacy."

BIBLIOGRAPHICAL ESSAY

Southeastern Archaeology

The southeastern quadrant of the United States is well endowed with the physical remains of ancient cultures. Rich in archaeological interest, the region was home to what Charles M. Hudson, in *The Southeastern Indians* [104, p. 78], has called "the highest cultural achievement . . . in all of North America." Jon D. Muller, "The Southeast" [136], is probably the best written and most accessible survey of southeastern prehistory. His description of the major sites and his interpretation of the cultures of the people who left them is sharp and clear, but he warns of the dangers of taking unwarranted liberties with the facts. Emphasizing the complexity of southeastern prehistory, Muller argues against the misleading tendency to generalize too glibly about the changes in cultural patterns between 10,000 B.C. and A.D. 1540—the period of demonstrable human occupation. He also advises against trying "to link prehistoric, archeologically defined societies with the 'historic' tribes of the Southeast." There were too many changes and too much mixing of people and cultures after the arrival of the Europeans to permit any clear tracing of lines between prehistoric cultural groups and historic political groups. Probably, he concedes, the present Creek Nation includes many people whose ancestors were members of the Dallas (Mississippian) society of eastern Tennessee, "but this is not the same as saying that the Dallas complex is prehistoric Creek."

Thomas M. N. Lewis and Madeline Kneberg, *Tribes That Slumber* [115], on the other hand, describes the Dallas and other prehistoric complexes and compares them with the cultural attributes of the historic tribes. The authors note, for example, that the council chamber in one of the ceremonial centers on Dallas Island "was almost identical in details to those of the historic Creek Indians" (p. 83).

Lewis and Kneberg refer to the people of the Dallas complex as living within the "temple mound" cultural tradition. The enormous and elaborate earthworks abounding in the Southeast have long attracted much scholarly attention, but few students of the "Mound Builders" have searched recent native communities for evidence of an ancient mound-building tradition. In "The Creek Indians as Mound Builders" [188], John R. Swanton shows that after little more than fifty years of use the dance grounds of the two Creek towns of Tuckabatchee and Kealidji, in Indian Territory, resembled in rudimentary form some of the mound complexes in Alabama and Georgia. The "constructions" resulted from the sweeping necessary to keep the ceremonial areas clean of debris and loose dirt. A raised oval ring around the edge was the dirt pile, and the mounds within, on which ceremonial buildings once sat, represented the original ground level before the "excavation" of hundreds of sweepings. So, Swanton concludes facetiously, the claim that the Creeks were once mound builders cannot be wholly ignored.

Much of the archaeological work in the Southeast is at historic sites. Historical evidence helps archaeologists interpret these sites, and the added dimension of archaeological evidence enriches the body of materials available to ethnohistorians as they attempt to understand the cultural history of southeastern native people.

In "Creek and Cherokee Culture in the Eighteenth Century" [172], William H. Sears uses archaeological evidence to test the migration legends of these two southeastern nations. By comparing historic Creek and Cherokee pottery styles with those of prehistoric residents, Sears argues that the Cherokees are indigenous to the southern Appalachian country, contrary to their legendary history. The Creeks, true to their legends, were intruders. Uncertain of its origins, Sears suggests that Creek culture developed in the Coosa valley of Alabama. It depends, he says, on which Creek group is considered. Writing with Gordon R. Willey, Sears elaborates on his Coosa origin thesis in "The Kasita Site" [208]. In both of these studies the crucial issue is to measure the difference or similarity between historic Creek and Cherokee pottery and that of the prehistoric people of north Georgia. Cherokee pottery styles clearly derive from Lamar, Sears contends; Creek design does not.

Charles H. Fairbanks, one of the most distinguished students of southeastern archaeology, shows in

"Creek and Pre-Creek" [61] how a talented scholar can use physical evidence to interpret historic culture change. The vast number of European artifacts unearthed at the sites of the Lower Creek towns of Cusseta, Coweta, Ocmulgee, and Oconee, occupied in the eighteenth century, suggests to Fairbanks that the Creeks moved with extraordinary speed to a "cash and barter economy." Such a transition, he argues, must have had radical effects on crafts, religion, economics, and diet. Further, he suspects a loss of community religious life. Fairbanks's evidence for such an interpretation lies in a comparison of pottery made in historic Ocmulgee with that made in the adjacent prehistoric Lamar site at Ocmulgee National Monument. The decorations are basically the same, but on the Ocmulgee pots they are sloppy, poorly delineated, and crude. Fairbanks speculates that the designs had specific meaning that the Lamar potters understood. Ocmulgee potters, on the other hand, were simply copying lines that meant nothing to them. This, concludes Fairbanks, suggests an erosion of Creek social and religious life that is directly related to the influx of European goods.

Carol I. Mason, in "Eighteenth Century Culture Change among the Lower Creeks" [122], also studied Ocmulgee pots. Striking to her was the large number of eighteenth-century potsherds in an archaeological "horizon" dominated by European artifacts. On the basis of this evidence, she argues that the fur trade had a much more profound effect on male Creeks than on female Creeks, whose lives remained relatively unchanged. Men purchased the tools and weapons they needed, but the women continued to make theirs. In the rapidly changing Creek world, women were the "force for cultural conservatism." Taken together, the articles by Fairbanks and Mason illustrate an interesting interpretive dichotomy. Studying Creek pots, Fairbanks notices the serious erosion of traditional Creek culture. Mason sees in those same pots "the thread of cultural continuity."

The European artifacts found in the towns of the Creek Confederacy have also been subjected to scholarly scrutiny, as have the trade patterns that brought them there. In two publications, *The Southern Indian Trade: Being Particularly a Study of Material from the Tallapoosa River Valley of Alabama* [26] and "Pensacola Indian Trade" [28], Peter A. Brannon describes the kinds of goods found in the market area of the Pensacola traders.

In "The Archaeology of European-Indian Contact in the Southeast" [91], David J. Hally describes the "state of the art" of historic archaeology as of 1971 and calls for more systematic excavation and analysis and more concern for the interpretation of local phenomena. "Creek," he argues, is a political, not a cultural concept. Rather than trying to identify and analyze Creek features, Hally calls for scholars to place their emphasis on the towns and study them as specific entities. Only that kind of foundation can render generalizations about Creek culture meaningful. The

Sears and Fairbanks articles illustrate the problem. Each uses Creek as his interpretive focus; but Sears says Creek pots do not follow the Lamar Complicated Stamped tradition, while Fairbanks says they do. Neither is mistaken; they are simply describing different cultures within a political institution that contained many cultural variations.

Creek Ethnography

Contemporary Creek people frequently call themselves Muskogees. Scholars rarely use the term in such a fashion, reserving it instead to refer to the Muskhogean language group and to the specific Muskogee language that most members of the Confederacy spoke. Language diversity characterized the Confederacy, however. In addition to the dominant Muskogee language, Alabama, Koasiti, Hitchiti, and Natchez—all Muskhogean languages—were spoken, as were the non-Muskhogean Yuchi and Shawnee. John R. Swanton, in "Aboriginal Culture of the Southeast" [192], cites this diversity to show the larger cultural complexity of the Southeast. Mary R. Haas, in "Southeastern Indian Linguistics" [88], goes further than Swanton by arguing that the Southeast may be nearly as linguistically diverse as California. No one would be more likely to know. As the author of well over a dozen publications in Creek linguistics, Haas has clearly dominated the field. Her article cited above, which includes a full bibliography, is the place to begin the study of that difficult subject.

Though old, three important additional sources should be consulted by anyone pursuing the study of the languages of the Creek Confederacy. James C. Pilling, *Bibliography of the Muskhogean Languages* [159], lists every item extant in 1889, published and unpublished, in any of the Muskhogean languages, along with sometimes rich bibliographical information on each reference. Robert M. Loughridge and David M. Hodge, *English and Muskogee Dictionary* [118], is the only published dictionary of the dominant language of the Confederacy. Henry F. Buckner's *A Grammar of the Maskwke or Creek Language* [29] is also essential for the linguist.

Albert S. Gatschet, *A Migration Legend of the Creek Indians, with a Linguistic, Historic and Ethnographic Introduction* [81], is one of the earliest attempts at a linguistic analysis of the Muskogee language within an ethnographic and historical context. Much more than an exercise in linguistics, this 1884 publication is also a strikingly modern-appearing experiment in combining historical sources with ethnographic fieldwork to produce a coherent cultural interpretation of the Creek Nation. Among other contributions, Gatschet persuasively argues that the appellation, Muskogee, long known to be a non-Muskogee word, is of Algonquian derivation, probably Shawnee, and refers, like *muskeg*, to a well-watered or swampy country. Ironically, the English term Creek, as shown by Verner W. Crane, "The Origin of the Name of the Creek Indians" [45], was used by the Carolina traders of Charles Town to distinguish the people who lived in the wet, marshy headwaters of the Ocmulgee River of north central Georgia. By the early eighteenth century, as these traders became better acquainted with the extent of the Confederacy, they enlarged the concept of "Creek" to include all those allied peoples.

The people thus named either Muskogee or Creek by others thought of themselves as neither. Rather, their identity as well as their loyalty was to their town. The word *talwa*, though generally translated as town, better refers to tribe and focuses our attention on the essential character of the Confederacy. As an association of separate, distinct, sovereign, and independent groups, the Confederacy was a loose gathering of tribes that maintained peace between its constituents and provided both a defensive security and a potential for allied offensive action. But each town retained its autonomy, and there is no known instance of an inter-town unity so complete as to suggest the existence of a Creek state. John R. Swanton, in "The Social Significance of the Creek Confederacy" [189, p. 332], argues, however, that it was a "nationality in the making, perhaps an empire." "The Creeks," he concludes, "had a true federal idea."

On the basis of the migration legends, Swanton believes the Confederacy was born before the first European penetration into North America. The earliest recorded account of Creek origins, printed without editorial analysis in Edgar Legare Pennington, ed., "Some Ancient Georgia Indian Lore" [155], was presented to General James Oglethorpe in 1735 as a series of pictographs painted on a white buffalo skin. Ex-

plained by Tchikilli, a headman of the Creek town of
Cusseta, the legend tells of the meeting, on a moun-
taintop far to the west, of the Cussetas, Alabamas,
Abihkas, and Chickasaws. The four nations allied, received fire and their chief medicines, established an
order of precedence, and marched east together. They
crossed many rivers, conquered and absorbed many
nations, and ultimately settled on the Chattahoochee
River, which now divides the states of Georgia and Alabama. From this central location the allies fanned
outward in all directions until they came to dominate,
at their greatest extent, virtually all of Georgia and Alabama, and Florida north of the Saint Johns River. Albert S. Gatschet, "Tchikilli's Kasi'hta Legend in the
Creek and Hitchiti Languages with a Critical Commentary and Full Glossaries to Both Texts" [82], along with
Gatschet's previously cited *Migration Legend,* provides
an extensive historical and ethnographic as well as linguistic analysis of the legend.

The history lesson Tchikilli delivered to Oglethorpe was properly the story of Cusseta and the role
of that tribe/town in the formation of the Confederacy.
It should therefore be compared with the origin
legends of the other towns, many of which are conveniently gathered in John R. Swanton's monumental
"Social Organization and Social Usages of the Indians
of the Creek Confederacy" [194]. Such a comparison
provides the necessary historical balance for a solid
understanding of the growth of the Confederacy; and,
more important, it holds our attention to the towns.

Morris E. Opler's "The Creek 'Town' and the Prob-

lem of Creek Indian Political Reorganization" [146] is
the premier interpretation of Creek towns. Based on
fieldwork done in the 1930s, Opler's essay analyzes the
town both as the traditional foundation upon which the
Confederacy rested and as the contemporary form of
social and political organization that commands the
first loyalty of most Creeks. In 1937, Opler identified
forty-four Creek towns in Oklahoma, twenty of which
still maintained a full roster of officials. The generally
accepted estimate of the number of Creek towns in the
eighteenth century is fifty to eighty. The large number
extant after thirty years of allotment suggests their importance in Creek life.

Much remains unknown about how towns related
to one another. The towns of the Confederacy were
divided in two ways, one of which was geographic. One
group, residing primarily in Georgia in the valleys of
the Chattahoochee, Flint, and Ocmulgee rivers, came
to be called by Anglo-Americans the Lower Towns.
Further west, "up" the trading road from Charles
Town on the Coosa, Tallapoosa, and Alabama rivers of
central Alabama, were the Upper Towns. Separated by
one hundred miles of densely forested country, these
two congregations of towns developed special local interests that sometimes brought them into verbal
conflict and often prevented harmonious cooperation
in the pursuit of a national policy. The physical separation of the Creeks into Upper Towns and Lower
Towns was perhaps as important as the principle of
town autonomy in preventing the centralization of the
Confederacy.

The towns were also divided into two sides or
"fires" designated by the colors white (or peace) and
red (or war). Swanton has developed the argument,
most vigorously presented in his "Social Organization
and Social Usages of the Indians of the Creek Confederacy" [194], that this division identified "related" and
"unrelated" towns and was most significant in deter-
mining which towns played ball against each other. Far
more than a sport, the intertown ball games, called by
the Creeks "the younger brother of war," provided
ways for young men to gain honors in time of peace
and, according to Swanton, supplied the machinery by
which foreign tribes were admitted into the Confederacy. Mary R. Haas, "Creek Inter-town Relations" [87],
interprets the ball game as the institution for channel-
ing Red/White animosities. Rival towns of opposite
"fires" formalized their antagonism by playing ball.
Alexander Spoehr, "Brief Communications" [180], cor-
roborates Haas's findings and suggests that the games
also served to preserve peace and solidarity among the
people of a single town.

As Spoehr pointed out in his "Changing Kinship
Systems: A Study in the Acculturation of the Creeks,
Cherokee, and Choctaw" [181], however, there were
many institutions in Creek life that sought to regulate
or influence interpersonal relationships. While the ball
game served an important function in intertown con-
tacts, within the towns the many-faceted clan organization defined the duties, obligations, and behavior
patterns of the Creeks. In the field in the 1930s,
Spoehr was struck by the degree to which Creeks re-

sisted acculturation, particularly when compared with the much less traditional Choctaws and Cherokees. The longevity of Creek social organization, Spoehr concluded, related to its formality and complexity. A strong clan structure bound by phratries and halved in moieties worked to keep the towns intact, and their equally complex series of town relationships within their respective "fires" carried the vitality beyond each locality into the Nation. The Creek design was far more elaborate than the Choctaw and Cherokee clan systems, and Spoehr demonstrated that its complexity kept it alive. This trio—Spoehr, Haas, and Opler—has set the stage for a badly needed but as yet unpublished analysis of contemporary Creek life.

While local particularism and town autonomy characterized the Creek Confederacy, there were important ceremonial events on the calendar that bound tighter the ties of alliance and kept the town friendships intact. None was more important, or more interesting to outside observers, than the annual "Green Corn Dance." Often referred to as the "Busk," a corruption of *pushkita,* which means "to fast," it is a four- or eight-day renewal celebration that has as its central element the extinguishing of the old fire and the kindling of the new. In conjunction with this ceremony, the clans gather to retell their history, the people dance and fast, and the town celebrates the first harvest of the season with a feast featuring green corn. Descriptions abound, one of the most fascinating being that written by John Howard Payne in 1835 and edited by John R. Swanton as "The Green Corn Dance" [195].

The standard ethnographic analysis of the Creek ceremonial cycle is John R. Swanton, "Religious Beliefs and Medical Practices of the Creek Indians" [193]. As the title suggests, this massive study is more than a description of Creek ceremonial life. By far the most extensive treatment of Creek medicine, in both its theoretical and its practical forms, this study is a rich compendium of historical description, ethnographic analysis, and field observations that underscores the inseparability of medicine and religion and demonstrates the influence of both on Creek daily life.

Swanton's "Social Organization and Social Usages of the Indians of the Creek Confederacy" [194] is the companion. Ethnographic in purpose, this monumental study rests solidly on a historical foundation. It stands, with Swanton's previously cited work on religion and medicine, as the indispensable introduction to any serious investigation of Creek ethnohistory.

In Elsie Clews Parsons, ed., *American Indian Life*, Swanton published "Tokulki of Tulsa" [191]. A fictional biography of a young man born into the Wind clan of the Creek town of Tulsa, this short piece shows with clarity and the insight of many years' experience how the beliefs and practices Swanton described clinically might have fit in a human setting. With a sensitivity rare among scholars, Swanton created in Tokulki the anthropologist's dream, the perfect specimen, and did it with such skill that one is tempted to think, for a moment, that life for a young precontact Creek may actually have been just as Swanton says.

Frank G. Speck, "The Creek Indians of Taskigi

Town" [176], is an important early study that focused on the culture of a particular town and points up the many exceptions to Swanton's generalizations. Speck also published "Ceremonial Songs of the Creeks and Yuchi Indians" [177]. One of the few sources for Creek songs, this gathering includes twenty-two dance songs and twenty medicine songs, most of which Speck analyzed. During the early 1880s, J. N. B. Hewitt had the opportunity to conduct several penetrating interviews with Legus C. Perryman and Pleasant Porter, both of whom later served as principal chiefs of the Creek Nation. In 1939, Swanton edited Hewitt's *Notes on the Creek Indians* [96], which, along with the editor's comments, supplies much additional detail on Creek political ethnohistory. Theodore C. Stern's "The Creeks" [182] is a very recent survey of Creek ethnology. John R. Swanton's *The Indians of the Southeastern United States* [196] and Charles M. Hudson's *The Southeastern Indians* [104] go far toward putting the Creeks into the larger perspective of the southeastern culture area.

In the forthcoming volume, *The Southeast* [65], now being prepared by Raymond D. Fogelson of the University of Chicago as volume 14 of *The Handbook of North American Indians,* there will be two articles of special interest to students of Creek ethnohistory. Willard Walker of Wesleyan University is writing the general article on the Creeks [205], and Rennard Strickland of the University of Tulsa is preparing the section on "The Five Civilized Tribes" [183]. Both promise to be excellent summaries of current knowledge.

Two early publications, though difficult to classify with precision, should probably be included in this commentary on ethnographic sources. James Adair's *The History of the American Indians* [5] was first published in 1775. A trader with several decades' residence among the Chickasaws, Adair was a thoughtful observer of southeastern Indian life. He became convinced that Native Americans were descended from the ten lost tribes of Israel and wrote this five-hundred-page book to prove it. Despite this bias, which is obvious and easily dismissed, the book is a mine of ethnographic and historical information on the southeastern nations, including the Creeks.

Louis LeClerc Milfort, *Memoirs; or, A Cursory Glance at my Different Travels and my Sojourn in the Creek Nation* [132], is a pack of historical lies mixed with many useful and accurate descriptions of Creek life. Particularly valuable are his accounts of Creek naming and war-preparation ceremonies. Milfort published the book in Paris in 1802 to support his claim to be the "war chief" of the Creek Confederacy, the chosen successor to Alexander McGillivray, and the man Napoleon should choose to lead the Creeks in forming a massive pro-French native alliance. Both Napoleon and historians saw through his claims, but careful ethnographic research has verified many of Milfort's observations, and the book has lived as a valuable, if somewhat untrustworthy source.

Henry Rowe Schoolcraft's *Historical and Statistical Information Respecting the History, Condition, and Prospects of the Indian Tribes of the United States* [171] is even more difficult to characterize. Published in six volumes between 1851 and 1857, it is an enormous but undigested mass of unorganized information. In 1954, Frances S. Nichols rendered it more usable by publishing her *Index to Schoolcraft's Indian Tribes of the United States* [141]. In preparation for its publication, Schoolcraft compiled a series of questions on a wide range of political, social, economic, religious, linguistic, and general topics that he mailed to people he considered knowledgeable within every native nation available to him. D. W. Eakins answered the questions for the Creeks in 1847, and Schoolcraft published his answers. Though lacking in coherence, this collection of responses is among the first deliberate ethnographic investigations of the Creeks and should not be overlooked.

This brief section by no means exhausts the anthropological literature on the Creeks. Students seeking additional sources should consult George P. Murdock and Timothy J. O'Leary, *Ethnographic Bibliography of North America* [137], volume 4.

Creek Historiography

General Studies

One cannot begin even a peripheral study of Creek history without early and continued excursions into Angie Debo's *The Road to Disappearance* [52]. The only extended Creek tribal history, it recounts the story of the Creeks from De Soto's *entrada* to allotment in the

early twentieth century. Written almost exclusively
from primary sources, Debo's book is a product of its
time. Its weaknesses—surprisingly few—lie not in
Debo's scholarship but rather in the paucity of Creek
ethnohistoriography in the 1930s. Despite that, her
analysis of Creek history, particularly in the postremoval period in Indian Territory, remains the standard by which other scholars must measure their work.
Donald E. Green's *The Creek People* [84] is a convenient
supplement to Debo. Much shorter, it has the twin
advantages of being thirty years more recent and including a brief section on the twentieth-century
postallotment experience of the Creeks in Oklahoma.
Muriel H. Wright's seventeen-page section on the
Creeks in her *A Guide to the Indian Tribes of Oklahoma*
[213] is the best short introduction to Creek history.

    While the Confederacy was, in a political sense at
least, more than the sum of its parts, the member tribes
that joined the alliance remained the building blocks of
the Nation. John R. Swanton's *Early History of the Creek
Indians and Their Neighbors* [190] is a series of brief historical descriptions of many of the towns (once tribes)
in the Confederacy plus most of the non-Creek tribes
that once lived in Georgia, Alabama, Mississippi, and
Florida. Like many of his publications, Swanton's *Early
History* contains a large quantity of unedited primary
material from very obscure early travel accounts, giving
it an added significance for students with limited access
to library materials. Swanton also provides an extended
analysis of nearly every early estimate of Creek popu-

lation, including the town-by-town census of 1832, the first complete enumeration of the Nation. The total was 21,733 (pp. 434–37).

Three other sources, each much shorter than Swanton's *Early History*, should be consulted for additional information on Creek towns. In order of value, they are Albert S. Gatschet, "Towns and Villages of the Creek Confederacy in the XVIII and XIX Centuries" [83]; Peter A. Brannon, "Aboriginal Towns in Alabama" [24]; and Thomas M. Owen, "Indian Tribes and Towns in Alabama" [149]. The special strengths of Gatschet's article are his ethnographic introduction and his inclusion of all known Creek towns. Brannon and Owen, primarily interested in the history of native people in Alabama, restricted their descriptive lists to that state.

Thomas M. Owen and his wife, Marie Bankhead Owen, were both active and prolific students of Alabama history. His "Alabama Indian Chiefs" [150] is a series of biographical sketches of many native leaders, mostly Creek, who were considered important to the history of Alabama. Taken from his massive four-volume history of Alabama published in the 1920s, this reprint makes much useful information more readily available. Mrs. Owen's "Indians in Alabama" [148] is a nearly unedited collection of all the material on the Creeks published in Frederick Webb Hodge's *Handbook of American Indians North of Mexico* [98]. Containing nothing new, her publication is useful primarily as a compendium.

Thomas L. McKenney and James T. Hall collaborated in publishing, during the 1840s, *History of the Indian Tribes of North America* [121], the finest collection of native portraits ever assembled. McKenney wrote a sketch, often several pages long, about each individual pictured. Several of these subjects were among the most influential Creeks of the early nineteenth century.

No study of Creek history after the 1780s can be done without some consideration of the relations between the Creeks and the United States. That history has been heavily influenced by the treaties signed by representatives of the two peoples. Seen by both sides as important milestones in their relations, the treaties described, among other things, the degree of Creek sovereignty the United States was willing to recognize, the boundaries of the Creek Nation, the services and cash the United States agreed to pay for land cessions, and the legal protections the Creeks had a right to expect in their daily contact with Whites. There are many published versions of these treaties, thirteen of which were made with the Creeks between 1790 and 1866, but the standard source is Charles J. Kappler, comp., *Indian Affairs, Laws and Treaties* [109], volume 2. C. J. Coley, "Creek Treaties, 1790– 1832" [37], is a brief summary of the treaties signed before removal.

It is dangerously easy for students of the Creeks (or any other nation) to forget the context of the events they seek to understand. Robert S. Cotterill, in *The Southern Indians: The Story of the Civilized Tribes Before Removal* [42], has performed a valuable service with his

combined analysis of the history of the Creeks, Choctaws, Chickasaws, Cherokees, and Seminoles before
about 1840. He interprets their relations with one another as well as their dealings, both individually and
collectively, with the many European and Euro-
American polities active in the Southeast. A careful
study of this unique volume will be rewarded by both
solid information and a sample of Cotterill's lively style.

Sixteenth and Seventeenth Centuries

Scholars know very little about the Creeks in the
sixteenth and seventeenth centuries. What little knowledge exists depends primarily on Spanish sources, with
a heavy emphasis on the accounts of explorations into
the southeastern interior in the sixteenth century. Of
these narratives, those of De Soto's *entrada* are the most
informative. While on the march for several years,
De Soto and his army spent nearly all of 1540 in the
Creek country. There are many translations of the accounts of their experiences; one conveniently accessible
paperbound edition is Buckingham Smith, trans., *Narratives of . . . De Soto in the Conquest of Florida* [173]. This
volume includes the narratives of "A Knight of Elvas"
and Luys Hernandez de Biedma. John R. Swanton,
"Ethnological Value of the DeSoto Narratives" [197],
evaluates the various accounts for ethnographic accu-
racy and suggests that their greatest significance lies in
their description of people who were still building
mounds.

Swanton's *The Indians of the Southeastern United States* [196], an ethnographic masterpiece, devotes the first several dozen pages to the early Spanish invasion accounts and their descriptions of early native life in the region.

David H. Corkran's *The Creek Frontier, 1540–1783* [39] has many strengths. Among them is perhaps the most complete discussion of Creek history in the sixteenth and seventeenth centuries one is likely to find. There are important supplements to it, however, one of which is Verner W. Crane, *The Southern Frontier, 1670–1732* [46], an excellent analysis of, among other things, the establishment and growth of Carolina-Creek relations. Herbert E. Bolton's "Spanish Resistance to the Carolina Traders in Western Georgia (1680–1704)" [19] is a careful interpretation of Spanish-English competition for Lower Creek trade and friendship. In attempting to maintain relations with both, the Creeks revealed in this episode the policy of playing both sides against each other that dominated their relations with all Europeans in the eighteenth century.

A quick glance through the volumes of the *Florida Historical Quarterly* and the *Georgia Historical Quarterly* will reveal a large number of articles on sixteenth- and seventeenth-century European activity in the Southeast. These studies tend to have a European focus, but the proximity of native people, including Creeks, assures that no careful analysis of settlement history will be without comment on European-Indian relations, and the student of Creek history during this period should refer to this material.

Eighteenth Century: Creeks and Europeans

The Southeast attracted many of the outstanding naturalists of the eighteenth century. It was an exotic country filled with strange animals and plants and inhabited by people who constantly roused the curiosity of scientific observers. Of the scholars who toured, studied, and wrote on the Southeast, the father-and-son team of John and William Bartram is among the most important to students of Creek history. The elder Bartram visited the Nation in the mid-1760s (John Bartram, "Diary of a Journey through the Carolinas, Georgia, and Florida from July 1, 1765, to April 10, 1766" [12]) and witnessed, among other things, the Treaty of Picoleta, 18 November 1765, between the British and the Lower Creeks that marked the East Florida boundary. His son William spent 1773 and 1774 in and around the Creek country (William Bartram, "Travels in Georgia and Florida, 1773–1774: A Report to Doctor John Fothergill" [13]). The Bartrams described the country, the towns, the people, and their institutions with the skill of trained scientists. William Bartram's observations and commentaries are especially informative. Published originally in two installments, 1789 and 1791, William Bartram, "Observations on the Creek and Cherokec Indians" [14], and

Travels of William Bartram, ed. Mark Van Doren [15], represented the mature reflections of a talented observer who spent many months visiting the Creeks and learning their history and way of life. Though the Bartrams describe the Creeks during the last half of the eighteenth century, there is a timelessness to their writings that will reward any thoughtful student of Creek history.

Albert James Pickett's *History of Alabama, and Incidentally of Georgia and Mississippi, from the Earliest Period* [158] is a good place to begin specific research on eighteenth-century Creek history, especially on Creek relations with their European neighbors. As one of the earliest modern scholarly historians of the Southeast, Pickett respected the Creeks, took their history seriously, and tried to understand and describe their pivotal role in the international competition for control of the region. This is an old study, and there was much Pickett did not know; but, on the other hand, much of the source material he used, especially interviews, has ceased to exist.

Pickett was particularly interested in the political institutions of the Creek Nation. Convinced that the Confederacy was unique to native America, he gave much attention to its policies. But, though he knew the last generation of Creek leaders in the East, he did not know very much about how the many councils worked, how decisions were made, or how policies were carried out. James F. Doster, *The Creek Indians and Their Florida Lands, 1740–1823* [57], has given us as clear an understanding of Creek political ethnohistory as we have. Doster shows how the National Council emerged during the eighteenth century as a political body that claimed and generally exercised control over the people and country on the southern periphery. Writing to support a Creek claim for a share in an Indian Claims Commission settlement in a Seminole case, Doster focused on the internal operation of the Confederacy government. This is the special strength of the book. Most scholars confine their research to the relations between native and European people.

Verner W. Crane, "The Origins of Georgia" [47], shifts the focus by discussing the international struggle for hegemony in the Southeast. Crane summarizes this competition in the 1730s as it related to the Creeks and points out that it was this conflict with Spain and France that stimulated England to establish Georgia.

Gen. James Oglethorpe, leader of Georgia during its early years, directed the colony's relations with the Creeks. They negotiated and signed two treaties, 1733 and 1739, that described the limits of Georgia's settlement, determined trade regulations, and generally put the relations between Georgia and the Creeks on a cooperative and harmonious level. These two treaties are printed in "Oglethorpe's Treaty with the Lower Creek Indians" [145]. E. Merton Coulter argues in "Mary Musgrove, 'Queen of the Creeks': A Chapter of Early Georgia Troubles" [43] that the secret of Oglethorpe's success with the Creeks lay in his using Mary Musgrove-Matthews-Bosomworth, niece of Brims, headman of Coweta and reputed "emperor" of the Lower Creeks, as his interpreter and advisor. As long as their relations were good, Coulter suggests, Georgia and the Creeks were friendly. When trouble came it was because Oglethorpe had returned to England and Mary's last husband, Thomas Bosomworth, prevailed on her to demand a large grant of land from Georgia. Coulter says it was a conspiracy to defraud the colony; John Pitts Corry, in "Some New Light on the Bosomworth Claims" [41], argues that Mary had a just claim to the lands in question, that Georgia's refusal to fully recognize her claim violated Creek custom, and that Mary's contribution to Georgia was such that the grant she demanded was reasonable compensation. Whether or not the land should have been Mary's, it is clear that this Creek woman, educated in Charles Town and married to a succession of English traders and ministers, was instrumental in cementing cordial Creek relations during the crucial early years of the colony's existence.

Corry's *Indian Affairs in Georgia, 1732–1756* [40] interprets Georgia's relations with the Creeks during the first half of its colonial life. It was a story of struggle between the ambitious Georgia settlers and the restraining trustees. Although growth occurred at a slower pace than under royal rule, the Creeks throughout this period were subject to the pressures of expansionist Englishmen. Corry concentrates on the Georgia side of the story and tells us disappointingly little about the Creek contribution to this period of political contact.

Daniel H. Thomas, "Fort Toulouse: The French

Outpost at the Alibamos on the Coosa" [199], is the history of the entry and development of French influence in the Creek Nation. Lasting roughly from 1715 to 1763, the French presence in the Nation was rarely more than a nuisance to the English and Spanish, but to the westernmost Upper Creeks the trade and friendship that centered at Fort Toulouse were of major importance. Situated near where Montgomery, Alabama, now stands, Fort Toulouse represented the third nation vying for control of the Southeast. British efforts to counteract this French influence among the Creeks are reported in Newton D. Mereness, *Travels in the American Colonies* [124], a collection of travel narratives that includes accounts of three eighteenth-century political excursions through the Creek Nation.

David H. Corkran's *The Creek Frontier, 1540–1783* [39] details the Creek response to this three-way struggle. Delicately balancing the forces, the Creeks insured that the three Europeans remained at about equal strength. With none strong enough to gain control and none weak enough to be destroyed, each was vulnerable and needed the aid of the Creeks to become dominant. The Creeks made promises, but they carefully avoided upsetting the balance.

The Creeks shared common borders with three European powers. The most dynamic boundary was on the Creek-English frontier in Georgia. Louis DeVorsey, Jr., a historical geographer, has demonstrated how useful a careful geographical analysis can be to the interpretation of a frontier situation. In his "Indian Boundaries in Colonial Georgia" [56], for example, DeVorsey traces the history of the eighteenth-century Creek-English frontier in Georgia. The two treaties of the 1730s limited Georgia's size, but the boundary was left informal. Only in 1763, after the British removed both the Spaniards and the French, was the frontier clearly determined.

During the 1760s and 1770s, with its role as a power broker ended, the Creek Nation sought to extend and regularize its trade relations with the British. The restraint of foreign competitors was gone, however, and the English exploited the opportunity. Settlers pushed across the border, traders raised their prices, and war threatened ("Thomas Campbell to Lord Deane Gordon: An Account of the Creek Nation, 1764" [31]). The Creeks fell deeply into debt and in 1773 gave up a large tract on the upper Savannah River to pay for the goods they had consumed. It was a heavy price, but the Creek people had come to depend on the trade. Indeed, as Homer Bast argues in "Creek Indian Affairs, 1775–1778" [16], trade opportunities greatly influenced Creek policy during the American Revolution. Early in the British-American conflict, Bast notes, both sides preferred that the Creeks remain neutral. Such a stance best suited the interests of the Nation, and until 1778 there was little pressure on the National Council to make a belligerent commitment. In 1778, when England sought an anti-American alliance, she threatened to end the trade unless the Creeks joined her. But, as Corkran, *The Creek Frontier* [39], and James H. O'Donnell, *Southern Indians in the American Revolution* [144], make clear, Creek participation in the American Revolution was not quite so automatic. Trade goods remained important, but they did not solely determine Creek policy. More significantly, the principle of town autonomy prevented the creation or execution of any unified national policy in the Revolutionary period.

Certainly, however, the British had more friends among the Creeks than did the Americans. John R. Alden shows in *John Stuart and the Southern Colonial Frontier: A Study of Indian Relations, War, Trade and Land Problems in the Southern Wilderness, 1754–1775* [6] that British Indian policy and its administration by Superintendent Stuart in the 1760s and 1770s provided protection from aggressive American frontiersmen that won native loyalty. Equally important, Stuart had talented agents. Alexander McGillivray, a Creek with mixed Scots and French ancestry, represented the British government in the Upper Towns throughout the war. Two scholars, Helen H. Tanner, in "Pipesmoke and Muskets: Florida Indian Intrigues of the Revolutionary Era" [198], and James H. O'Donnell, in "Alexander McGillivray: Training for Leadership, 1777–1783" [143], have recently concluded that McGillivray's contribution to the British war effort among the Creeks was enormous.

Peace, Prosperity and Peril: 1783–1813

Alexander McGillivray turned out to be much more than a functionary in the British Indian service. By the time the Revolutionary War was over this young man, about twenty-four years old in 1783, had emerged as an important advisor and interpreter to the headmen of the Creek National Council. He recommended that the Creeks return to the power-broker policy of the mid-eighteenth century and that they balance the Spanish and American influence in the Southeast and thus buy time for the Confederacy to strengthen itself so it could stand alone to defend its territorial integrity and political independence. It was an enormously difficult task, demanding a rare degree of diplomatic skill, and for a time McGillivray was successful.

There was much about McGillivray that made him unusual, but it was his literacy that determined his role in history. He was the only Creek before the late nineteenth century to leave behind a collection of manuscripts. Arthur P. Whitaker, long a leading student of the diplomatic history of the Southeast, found a cache of McGillivray letters in the Spanish archives. Beginning with his "Alexander McGillivray, 1783–1793" [207], published in 1928, scholars have leaned heavily on the McGillivray material, producing a seemingly endless stream of studies that depend, at least in part, on his unique Native American perspective.

Whitaker interpreted McGillivray as a "half-breed"—a "bizarre confusion of sophistication and primative illogicality" who suffered from "psychic dualism" and "emotional instability." The evidence Whitaker used to support this judgment shows McGillivray playing the Spanish and Americans against one another while simultaneously trying to maintain a steady flow of trade. Whitaker, who saw McGillivray's preoccupation with trade as proof of his selfishness, had no conception of trade's role in intersocietal relations and failed to appreciate its political and economic importance to the Creek Nation.

A decade later, John Caughey published *McGillivray of the Creeks* [33]. With a short biographical introduction, this volume is primarily McGillivray's correspondence translated, edited, and printed. Not an exhaustive collection of McGillivray letters, Caughey's *McGillivray* should be supplemented with D. C. Crobitt, trans. and ed., "Papers Relating to the Georgia-Florida Frontier, 1784–1800" [38].

Like Whitaker, Caughey interprets McGillivray largely in an international context. Caughey's McGillivray is not much interested in or involved with domestic affairs. He is preeminently a diplomat negotiating with the Spanish, reacting to the Americans, and acting out some kind of personal role that seems to have no context beyond trade interests. In his "Alexander McGillivray and the Creek Crisis, 1783–1784" [32], Caughey describes how the Creek-Spanish alliance of 1784 came from McGillivray's desire to guarantee a regular trade in the uncertain postwar period. Arthur Orrmont, *Diplomat in Warpaint: Chief Alexander McGillivray of the Creeks* [147], is a popularized reworking of this Whitaker-Caughey thesis that perpetuates the assumption that McGillivray had no important Creek roots. William C. Sturtevant, in his "Commentary" [185], is perhaps the most recent proponent of the interpretation that McGillivray, like other mixed-blood "culture brokers" in other native communities, was not really a participant in Creek society.

The importance of McGillivray in the diplomatic setting of the Southeast cannot be denied. He signed a treaty with the Spanish at Pensacola in 1784 that, according to Jack D. L. Holmes, "Spanish Treaties with West Florida Indians, 1784–1802" [101], accomplished Spain's goal of erecting the southern Indian nations as buffers to protect Florida from American expansion. Lawrence Kinnaird, "International Rivalry in Creek Country, Part I: The Ascendancy of Alexander McGillivray, 1783–1789" [111], argues that stability in the Southeast depended on McGillivray, who would hold the Creeks to a Spanish alliance as long as the trade through Panton, Leslie and Company, a British firm operating out of Saint Augustine and Pensacola on a Spanish license, was satisfactory. In his "Creek-American Relations, 1782–1790" [58], Randolph C. Downes shows how the United States under the Articles of Confederation government could not restrain Georgia and establish a relationship with the Creeks friendly enough to drive a wedge between them and

Spain. McGillivray remained open to American offers, but, as Lucia Burk Kinnaird demonstrates in "The Rock Landing Conference of 1789" [112], he expected to be treated with dignity and intelligence and would not hesitate to suspend talks if he believed he was being insulted. It was in his ultimate best interests to make peace with the United States, however, and, as J. Leitch Wright, Jr., points out in "Creek-American Treaty of 1790: Alexander McGillivray and the Diplomacy of the Old Southwest" [211], the Treaty of New York was generally favorable to the Creeks. But factional opposition to the treaty weakened McGillivray, and by the time of his death in 1793, his relations with both the United States and Spain were strained and getting worse. Randolph C. Downes shows in "Creek-American Relations, 1790–1795" [59] that, if the United States had not already been bogged down in a war with the Indians north of the Ohio River, it would probably have invaded the Creek Nation in 1792 to force compliance with the treaty of 1790.

I have argued elsewhere (Michael D. Green, "Alexander McGillivray" [86]) that this concentration on McGillivray's relations with Spain and the United States distorts the significance of McGillivray as a Creek leader. Called by the Creeks *Isti atcagagi thlacco* (Great Beloved Man), McGillivray was primarily interested in strengthening the Confederacy from within. He imposed an unprecedented degree of centralized political leadership, trying to subordinate towns, eradicate factionalism, and unify the great potential strength of the

Nation so it could successfully withstand the pressures
of outside forces. Caleb Swan, who wrote "Position and
State of Manners and Arts in the Creek, or Muscogee
Nation in 1791" [187], and John A. Pope, who wrote *A
Tour through the Southern and Western Territories of the
United States of North-America; the Spanish Dominions on
the River Mississippi, and the Floridas; the Countries of the
Creek Nations; and Many Uninhabited Parts* [160], both
knew McGillivray and understood what he was doing,
and they describe something of his dreams for a viable
Creek Nation.

McGillivray died in 1793 at the age of thirty-four.
There was no one in the Nation who was capable of
filling his place, but at least two men sought his position. Carolyn Thomas Foreman has tried to describe
one of these hopefuls in "The White Lieutenant and
Some of His Contemporaries" [71]. Also known as
Fushatchee Mico, the Birdtail King of Okfuskee, the
White Lieutenant became for a while a key spokesman
of the National Council, but he never approached
McGillivray in talent or influence. The other hopeful
has been fully interpreted by J. Leitch Wright in
*William Augustus Bowles; Director General of the Creek Na-
tion* [212]. Bowles was a strange, colorful, almost
storybook character who slipped in and out of Creek
history between 1788 and 1803, fishing in whatever
troubled waters he could find and anxious to elevate
himself to some sort of exalted position. The historical
literature on Bowles is extensive, but his impact on the
Creeks was minimal.

The year after the Treaty of New York, the United States appointed James Seagrove, a trader from Georgia, to the new position of federal agent to the Creek Nation. Seagrove was in office from 1791 to 1795, and his duties included enforcing the provisions of the Creek treaty of 1790, keeping Creek warriors out of the war in the Ohio country, and eradicating Spanish influence. Seagrove was afraid of the Creeks—so much so that while McGillivray was alive he would not enter the Nation. Things changed in 1793. Not only did McGillivray die, but Georgia stepped up her harassment of the frontier. Gen. John Twiggs's "The Creek Troubles of 1793" [202] includes letters from the Georgia militia command planning a major invasion of the Creek Nation in hopes of conquering the country west of the Oconee River. Daniel M. Smith, "James Seagrove and the Mission to Tuckaubarchee, 1793" [174], describes Seagrove's efforts to calm the Creeks and keep the peace between them and Georgia. Overcoming his fears, the agent journeyed into the Upper Towns in the fall of 1793 and stayed the winter, vastly strengthening United States relations with the Creeks.

Seagrove was so successful that the alarmed Spaniards sent John Hambly, a secret agent from near Saint Augustine, on three missions into the Creek Nation. Richard K. Murdock, ed., "Mission to the Creek Nation in 1794" [138], and Daniel J. J. Ross and Bruce S. Chappell, eds., "Visit to the Indian Nations: The Diary of John Hambly" [168], describe Hambly's attempts to sabotage Seagrove, undercut United States influence, and recover for Spain a dominant position in Creek affairs of state. Hambly returned to Florida at the end of 1794, having failed to dislodge the Anglo-Americans.

Seagrove was replaced in 1795 by Benjamin Hawkins. No non-Creek in the history of the Nation ever wielded such influence or played such a decisive role in Creek affairs as Hawkins. Indeed, Merritt B. Pound, Hawkins's chief biographer, has suggested that Hawkins should perhaps be considered McGillivray's successor as the Great Beloved Man of the Creeks.

In two short summaries, "Benjamin Hawkins" [164] and "Benjamin Hawkins, Indian Agent" [162], and in one full-length biography, *Benjamin Hawkins, Indian Agent* [163], Pound has told Hawkins's story. A well-born and highly educated North Carolinian, Hawkins served in the 1780s on several congressional Indian commissions. He became acquainted with McGillivray and the Creeks and developed an interest in "civilizing" them through continuing the reforms of government begun by McGillivray and through introducing spinning, weaving, and scientific farming. Frank L. Owsley, Jr., in "Benjamin Hawkins: The First Modern Indian Agent" [151], argues that Hawkins was the first Indian agent to use these "modern" techniques to assimilate the Creeks.

Hawkins left behind an unusually rich collection of primary source material, much of which has been published by the Georgia Historical Society. In particular, see his *A Sketch of the Creek Country in the Years 1798 and*

1799 [94]. His personal account of an extended tour through the Nation, the *Sketch* is a fascinating description of the Creek people, their towns, and much of their history. To supplement the *Sketch* see *Letters of Benjamin Hawkins, 1796–1806* [95], an invaluable collection of Hawkins's correspondence for the first decade of his tenure as Creek agent.

In the early 1790s, at about the same time that the Washington administration began systematically to appoint federal Indian agents, President Washington also suggested the government trading system. As designed by Congress, this entailed the establishment and operation of a number of trading posts where federal officers would engage in trade with native people. Called factories, these stores were located in areas where they could be useful in competition with foreign traders. The federal government built the first factory among the Creeks in the hope that they would become dependent on the United States rather than the Spanish for their trade goods. In "The Creek Trading House—From Coleraine to Fort Hawkins" [123], Ray H. Mattison has written the history of the Creek factories in Georgia. Closed during the War of 1812, the postwar operation was resumed in Alabama. Nella J. Chambers, "The Creek Indian Factory at Fort Mitchell" [35], concludes the history of the Creek factories.

It was hard for the factories to overcome the influence of the private traders, especially those who operated out of Spanish Florida. Since 1784 the Spanish had permitted a select group of British traders to monopolize commerce with the southeastern natives, and an intimate relationship had developed. It was a connection with mutual benefits and obligations built on a system of credit. The factories, prohibited by Congress from extending credit to native customers, found that cheaper prices could not break the ties that credit bound. "The Creek Nation, Debtor to John Forbes and Company, Successors to Panton, Leslie and Company. A Journal of John Innerarity, 1812" [105], details the trade on the eve of the War of 1812 and describes how the Creek National Council conducted the economic affairs of the Confederacy.

The Creek War

Innerarity made no mention of it, but, in 1812 when he was in the Nation, the Creeks were deeply divided in a factional conflict that became, within a year, civil war. Theron A. Nuñez, Jr., "Creek Nativism and the Creek War of 1813–1814" [142], says that forced acculturation caused the trouble. Hawkins pressed his "civilization" policy, settlers encroached on Creek lands, and the more isolated Upper Towns were thrust into sudden contact with Whites. These cultural tensions spawned a prophetic movement that espoused nativism and embraced the teachings of Tecumseh and his brother, the Shawnee Prophet. It was a classic revitalization movement as described byAnthony F. C. Wallace and, as Nuñez argues, the issues were Creek. It was accidental that this civil conflict became war and involved Whites.

Nuñez's interpretation is interesting, especially in its use of Wallace's analytical model to put the Creek experience into perspective. The appendix to Nuñez's article is as valuable as the text. He printed in full his major source, George Stiggins's narrative history of the Creeks. Focusing on the period of the civil war, the Stiggins narrative describes the events of the years before the outbreak of violence with a particular emphasis on institutional history. A citizen of the Confederacy himself, Stiggins was in a unique position to describe and explain the history of his people, and it is to be profoundly regretted that he failed to extend his commentary beyond about 1815.

The civil war became the Creek War in 1813. Ethnohistorians have never fully analyzed how the transformation occurred, but students of the southeastern frontier have constructed a scenario that charts the course of events. "A Prelude to the Creek War of 1813–1814," ed., Elizabeth Howard West [106], is a series of letters from John Innerarity to his brother that describes the arrival in Pensacola of a group of Creek warriors loyal to the nativist prophets. Bullying the Spanish commandant into giving them a large amount of ammunition, they headed north to use it against their opponents, the Anglicized Creeks. A force of Creek mixed-bloods and Mississippi militia ambushed the nativists on their way home, stole the ammunition, and fortified themselves at several stockaded homes. One of these places, the house of Samuel Mims, became the site of a battle that gave land-hungry Tennesseans like Andrew Jackson the excuse they needed to wage a "just war" against the Creeks. Frank L. Owsley, Jr., "The Fort Mims Massacre" [153], is only the latest of a string of articles on that unfortunate event. The nativist Creek warriors killed almost everybody within the stockade at Mims's place, either directly or by firing the buildings. The estimated number of victims varies widely, but the minimum figure seems to have been about 260.

Many of those who died at Fort Mims were Creeks, and there is much historical reason for arguing that this, like earlier acts of violence, was a Creek affair that should not have involved outsiders. For those looking for an excuse to intervene in Creek business, however, the presence of non-Creeks at Fort Mims provided a perfect justification. As James F. Doster shows in *The Creek Indians and Their Florida Lands, 1740–1823* [57], Andrew Jackson and his Tennessee friends needed only the tiniest excuse. And the intervention came not just from Tennessee but from Mississippi and Georgia as well. Peter A. Brannon, ed., "Journal of James A. Tait for the Year 1813" [25], and John Floyd, "Letters of John Floyd, 1813–1838" [64] are only two of many sources on the Georgia invasion.

As James W. Holland, "Andrew Jackson and the Creek War: Victory at the Horseshoe" [100], points out, Jackson had no particular battle plan, and the Creek War had no tactical coherence. It was, in Holland's words, a series of "search and destroy missions," with the last battle fought in March 1814 at the Horseshoe Bend of the Tallapoosa River in eastern Alabama.

The best short interpretation of the war is Arthur

H. Hall, "The Red Stick War: Creek Indian Affairs during the War of 1812" [90]. Influenced by postremoval Creek history, Hall sees the Creek War as a fairly clear conflict between traditionalists and progressives. A fuller analysis is Henry S. Halbert and T. H. Ball, *The Creek War of 1813 and 1814* [89]. More sophisticated than Hall, Halbert and Ball discuss at length the origins of the Creek civil conflict and argue that the Whites grossly overreacted to the Fort Mims episode. The Tennesseans especially, but the Georgians and Mississippians as well, jumped at the excuse offered by Fort Mims to wage a "war of extermination" to get land. The physical damage was staggering. Halbert and Ball document nearly three thousand nativist Creeks dead. Out of this carnage came the Treaty of Fort Jackson, dictated in August 1814 by Andrew Jackson to the "loyal" Creek side of the civil conflict, which extorted from the Nation twenty-five million acres of land in Alabama and southern Georgia.

Most of the published works on the Creek War were done a generation ago. Ross Hassig, "Internal Conflict in the Creek War of 1813–1814" [93], almost the only recent study, is an attempt to identify the factors that influenced Creeks to align against each other in civil strife. After evaluating and discarding the traditional explanations, Hassig concludes that the conflict was generally along age lines. His most important argument, however, is that the adaptability of the Creek sociopolitical structure was such that the civil war was not very disruptive—it was certainly not beyond the bounds of allowable conflict—and if the Whites had not intervened the Creeks could have peacefully and easily reintegrated themselves.

Removal

Thomas S. Woodward entered the Creek Nation in 1813 as a soldier in the Georgia army. He stayed in Alabama after the Creek War and became one of the growing number of frontiersmen who lived with a foot on each side of the border. In the late 1850s, in his old age, Woodward enjoyed regaling the Montgomery newspaper-reading public with his *Reminiscences of the Creek, or Muscogee Indians, Contained in Letters to Friends in Georgia and Alabama* [210]. Written mainly from memory, Woodward's *Reminiscences* are rich in Creek local color. He knew nearly all the prominent Upper Creek families and recorded the genealogies of most of them. It is a fascinating volume; the style is informal, and Woodward emerges as an engaging old curmudgeon. Careful research has disclosed many errors, however, and Woodward, though essential, must be used with great care.

One of Woodward's favorite Creeks was William McIntosh. A prominent Coweta headman and commander of the Creek forces allied with Jackson during the Creek War, McIntosh assumed a dominant position in the postwar National Council. But he was willing, even anxious, to sell his influence to government officials. McIntosh thus became an active participant in treaty negotiations in the late 1810s and the 1820s. On his advice the Creeks sold land to the United States in 1818, 1821, and 1825, and on each occasion McIntosh received a handsome reward. James C. Bonner has argued in "Tustunugee Hutkee and Creek Factionalism on the Georgia-Alabama Frontier" [20] and in "William McIntosh" [21] that McIntosh represented a fairly large group of Creek mixed-bloods whose influence in the Nation was exerted most often on the side of the Whites. These Lower Creeks were receptive to White culture, Christianity, and European dress and agriculture and were part of the White money economy. The Upper Creeks, Bonner argues, tended to be more "primitive" and full-blooded and were highly opposed to the Anglicization of their culture. This oversimplifies Bonner's analysis somewhat. It seems clear, however, that McIntosh represented a pattern of thinking that, as it related to selling land to the United States, characterized a smaller mixed-blood group of Lower Creeks than Bonner recognizes.

On 12 February 1825, McIntosh and a handful of friends signed the Treaty of Indian Springs. In this document the Creek Nation gave up all its lands in Georgia and half its holdings in Alabama. It was a fraudulent treaty, signed against the will of all of the most prominent Creek leaders and agreed to by McIntosh despite a law of the council that provided the death penalty for the unauthorized selling of land. The United States Senate ratified the treaty early in March

1825; within two months a body of Creek warriors exe-
cuted McIntosh and two others who had violated the
law by signing the treaty. The number of accounts of
McIntosh's death is overwhelming. Most, however, call
it assassination and bitterly denounce the "savages"
who killed him in the name of a "primitive" government with "barbaric" laws. Bonner, in the two articles
previously cited, knows it was a legal execution.

The Creeks had begun in 1818 to draft a national
code. The earliest known copy of their laws, written
early in January 1825 by Chilly McIntosh, the son of
William McIntosh, is published in Antonio J. Waring,
Laws of the Creek Nation [206], along with a penetrating
interpretation of McIntosh and the political climate in
Georgia as it related to the Creeks.

Georgia had long been the nemesis of the Creeks,
and during these middle years of the 1820s that state
kept life miserable for them. It is an extremely complicated story, the outline of which can be found in Ulrich
Bonnell Phillips, *Georgia and States Rights: A Study of the
Political History of Georgia from the Revolution to the Civil
War, with Particular Regard to Federal Relations* [157]. A
pioneering study by one of the leading students of the
history of the South, *Georgia and States Rights* should be
read with the realization that it has a clear states-rights
bias that tends to blur the failures of the federal government to protect the Creeks from state harassment.
Two articles by Richard J. Hryniewicki, "The Creek
Treaty of Washington, 1826" [102] and "The Creek
Treaty of November 15, 1827" [103], detail the story of

how the Treaty of Indian Springs was abrogated and these two documents negotiated to stand in its place. The outcome was the same—the ouster of the Creeks from Georgia. Thomas L. McKenney, head of the Office of Indian Affairs, participated in both and conducted the negotiations for the 1827 pact. His assessment of this "Creek crisis" is in his *Memoirs, Official and Personal: With Sketches of Travels among the Northern and Southern Indians* [120]. James C. Bonner, ed., "Journal of a Mission to Georgia in 1827" [22], is the fascinating diary of a young army lieutenant who carried secret dispatches from the Indian Office to the Georgia governor.

When the United States negotiated with the Creeks in the 1820s, it hoped they would remove to the far west. They left Georgia but went no farther than Alabama, the eastern portion of which they continued to claim and hold. Theodore H. Jack, "Alabama and the Federal Government: The Creek Indian Controversy" [107], gives a picture of Alabama's outraged response to the influx of some ten thousand Creek refugees. The bias of Jack's article is clear in his title—the presence of Creeks in Alabama was a crisis in federal-state relations. Other scholars have followed this view by ignoring the more difficult question of what was happening to the Creeks. Thomas C. McCorvey, "The Mission of Francis Scott Key to Alabama in 1833" [119], recounts the story of how President Jackson sent Key to work out a peaceful settlement with Alabama that would remove the Creeks and retain the solid Jackson majorities in the state electorate. Frank L. Owsley, Jr., "Francis Scott Key's Mission to Alabama in 1833" [152], tells the story again, a little more critically.

Michael D. Green, "Federal-State Conflict in the Administration of Indian Policy: Georgia, Alabama, and the Creeks, 1824–1834" [85], is the most recent of these policy studies. Though more comprehensive than the others, it suffers from the same weakness of focus. The federal-state conflict, very real in both the Georgia and Alabama situations, has been fully analyzed. What remains to be told is the story of the Creeks in this period.

The treaty of 1832 included a provision for the allotment of reserves to Creek heads of families who chose to reside in Alabama. There was a delay in the survey and assignment of these reserves, but by mid-1834 the allotment was completed. According to the treaty, the Creek reservee could sell his tract under the supervision of special federal officers. Mary E. Young, "The Creek Frauds: A Study in Conscience and Corruption" [215], describes how the policy was perverted to benefit speculators and cheat the Creeks of both their lands and the money. The Creek situation was not unique, as Young shows in *Redskins, Ruffleshirts and Rednecks: Indian Allotments in Alabama and Mississippi, 1830–1860* [216], a comparative study of the Creek, Choctaw, and Chickasaw experiences.

The land frauds of the mid-1830s, coupled with the influx of several thousand settlers, made miserable the last years of the Creeks in Alabama. There were several swindles, and it was virtually impossible to avoid them. As the pressures to remove increased, frustrated and outraged Creeks struck out against their White tormentors. There were a few incidents that the Alabama legislature interpreted as a war. General Thomas S. Jesup of the United States Army arrived, took command of the Alabama militia, and rounded up thousands of Creeks for removal. John A. Campbell, "The Creek War of 1836" [30], and Peter A. Brannon, "Creek Indian War, 1836–37" [27], both describe this conflict.

The trouble in Alabama flared from the frustration of the Creeks who resisted moving west and who resented the harassment they received in the East. It is difficult to determine with absolute precision who these Creeks were, except to say that they were the vast majority of the whole population of both Upper and Lower Towns. The McIntosh faction, those who had supported William McIntosh in the early 1820s in his efforts to sell the eastern territory of the Creek Nation, had numbered only a few hundred, mostly from the Lower Town of Coweta. McIntosh's execution had frightened his friends and relatives, and they fled to Indian Territory. During the winter of 1827–28 some six hundred of them trekked west under the guidance of a removal agent appointed by the federal government. The Treaty of 1826 encouraged individual removal, and by 1829 more than twelve hundred Creeks hostile to the McIntosh group had also migrated. These, along with another six hundred who joined the

McIntosh people, created a series of settlements on the Arkansas and Verdigris rivers in present eastern Oklahoma. Not much scholarship has been published on this early movement of Creeks to Indian Territory. The best study is chapter 20 of Grant Foreman's *Indians and Pioneers: The Story of the American Southwest before 1830* [74]. Foreman shows that federal tardiness in providing promised protection in Georgia and Alabama was paralleled by a similar refusal to supply the emigrant Creeks with the stipulated traps, guns, blankets, and seed, and with protection from the "wild tribes" of the Plains.

This voluntary removal (voluntary only to distinguish it from the forced marches of later years) occurred because of certain financial promises and other encouragements extended over the previous several years by the United States government. After the War of 1812, the pressure from the states to hasten the speed of removal increased, and in a variety of fairly subtle ways the federal government responded. But the dedication of the administrations of James Madison, James Monroe, and even John Quincy Adams to the policy of Indian removal was never strong enough to satisfy White frontier interests. Tension between national policy and local impatience was the central element in the federal-state conflict that soured Georgia's and Alabama's relations with Washington. Then, after 1830, the quality of removal changed and volunteerism was no longer assumed. The classic analysis of the history of the removal idea, its legislative, administrative, and judicial proceedings, and particularly the effects of the 1830 Indian Removal Act is presented by Annie Heloise Abel in "The History of Events Resulting in Indian Consolidation West of the Mississippi" [1].

Grant Foreman has studied the process of removal for each of the five southeastern nations in *Indian Removal: The Emigration of the Five Civilized Tribes of Indians* [75]. His section on the Creeks is the most complete treatment of the subject extant.

Resettlement in Indian Territory

Grant Foreman was a prolific student of the history of Indian Territory, and most of his books are important for Creek history. *The Five Civilized Tribes* [77], a sequel to his study of removal, is a history of the re-creation of native societies in Indian Territory after the removal experience. With a section for each of the five southeastern nations, this volume includes a seventy-five-page summary of Creek history from 1830 to 1860.

William W. Savage, Jr., "Creek Colonization in Oklahoma" [170], is a useful corollary to Foreman's study. Savage argues that factionalism has been the key fact of Creek life since early in the eighteenth century. The troubles in the 1820s, including the execution of McIntosh, were simply one more manifestation of this continuing problem. By the mid-1830s the McIntosh progressives, having been in Indian Territory nearly a decade, were well on their way toward economic prosperity. Then into their midst came many thousand starving conservatives from Alabama. For the next several decades, Savage contends, this progressive-conservative division within Creek society perpetuated the factionalism that had so long characterized Creek politics.

When the main body of Creeks arrived among the western Creek Nation late in 1836, they were in desperate condition. More than thirty-five hundred died within a year of their arrival, and those who survived lived in extreme poverty. The government thought it had made adequate provision for the migration and was surprised by the enormous suffering. Immediately the question of fraud arose, and early in the 1840s Major General Ethan Allen Hitchcock was dispatched to Indian Territory to investigate. Grant Foreman edited his journal: *A Traveler in Indian Territory: The Journal of Ethan Allen Hitchcock, Late Major-General in the United States Army* [78]. Hitchcock spent several months with the Creeks, found abundant evidence of fraud on the part of many government removal and subsistence officers, and also recorded a great deal of information on the condition of the Creeks in 1842. He was particularly interested in their laws, which he described in some detail.

One question of concern to Hitchcock and other government officials was the relationship between the Creeks and other eastern Indians and the "wild" tribes of the Plains into whose country the easterners had been thrust. Many western nations, especially the Osages, bitterly resented the influx of so many thousand strangers. In *Advancing the Frontier, 1830–1860* [76], Grant Foreman studied this question. The emigrant nations, he found, were generally anxious to create and maintain peaceful relations with their western brothers, and the Creeks, especially, sought out opportunities to meet and discuss common problems. The Creeks hosted two large international conferences at Okmulgee in the 1840s where delegations from most of the South Plains tribes met with headmen of the easterners to make peace. Foreman praises the Creeks for their efforts and is sharply critical of the United States for doing little beyond what "expediency" demanded to maintain peace in Indian Territory.

Most of the published material on the western Creeks before 1860 can be categorized in two groups: missions and genealogy. It is a mission history of slow beginnings in Georgia and Alabama, documented by Carolyn Thomas Foreman in "Lee Compere and the Creek Indians" [72] and by Joseph G. Smoot, ed., in "An Account of Alabama Indian Missions and Presbyterian Churches in 1828 from the Travel Diary of William S. Potts" [175], and it suggests that preremoval Creeks had little interest in Christianity. The prospects for evangelism were even more bleak in Indian Territory. In the late 1830s the Creek National Council, in a series of decisions, forbade preaching and ordered all ministers expelled from the Nation. Creek Christians worshiped surreptitiously or crossed into the Cherokee

Nation for services. As Roland Hinds, "Early Creek Missions" [97], shows, it was only in 1844, after two prominent Creeks, Roley McIntosh and Ben Marshall, asked for a preacher that the council rescinded its ban. The Reverend R. M. Loughridge stood out as the most active and influential early missionary. Carolyn Thomas Foreman's "Report of the Reverend R. M. Loughridge to the Board of Foreign Missions Regarding the Creek Mission" [69] tells the institutional history of the major mission operations in the 1840s and 1850s. Loughridge's two stations, Coweta and Tullahassee, have been recalled in two articles. Augustus W. Loomis, "Scenes in the Indian Territory: Kowetah Mission" [117], is a reprint of a description first published in 1851 by the "Christian Commander" of Fort Gibson. Mostly anecdotal, Loomis's description does include some information on the school regimen. Virginia E. Lauderdale published "Tullahassee Mission" [114] in 1948. By far the most influential mission in the Nation, Tullahassee counted among its graduates many of the Creek leaders of the nineteenth century.

In addition to their religious and educational functions, the missionaries also helped preserve the Creek language in written form. In 1835 they began a publishing enterprise that turned out children's books. Guy Logsdon, "Oklahoma's First Book: 'Istutsi in Naktsoku,' by John Fleming" [116], describes the several Creek-language books published in the 1830s under the auspices of the American Board of Commissioners for Foreign Missions.

The biographical or genealogical material is a mixed bag. Some individuals were enormously influential and deserve serious study that they have not received, whereas others appear simply to have left behind a proud descendant. John Bartlett Meserve has written a large number of biographical sketches, two of which: "Chief Opothleyahola" [125] and "The MacIntoshes" [128], are worth considering because the subjects are so important. Carolyn Thomas Foreman, "A Creek Pioneer: Notes concerning 'Aunt Sue' Rogers and Her Family" [67], is a McIntosh genealogy. And William A. Sapulpa's "Sapulpa" [169] is a fond memorial to a forebear.

André Paul DuChateau, "The Creek Nation on the Eve of Civil War" [60], is a careful but brief account of the economic, social, and political situation in the Creek Nation in the late 1850s. In addition to a "state of the nation" style of economic and political summary, DuChateau has some interesting comments on Creek culture. It was changing, he says, but at different rates in different communities, depending on their mixed- or full-blood status. Neither group had a culture that could provide for all the needs of the people, DuChateau argues, which meant that some form of cultural rationalization was necessary to harmonize the factions and to prepare them for the future. He suggests that this was happening when the "final tragedy," Creek involvement in the United States Civil War, occurred.

The United States Civil War

In the historiography of the Civil War, Indian Territory is frequently forgotten. It was not overlooked in 1861, however. Indian Territory's great strategic importance as a buffer for Texas was obvious to the Confederacy. Annie Heloise Abel published under the title, *The Slaveholding Indians* [2–4], the definitive history of the Civil War in Indian Territory. In this three-volume work, Abel devoted a book each to prewar diplomacy, the war, and Reconstruction. Any student of Creek history beginning research on the era of the Civil War should consult Abel first. A general study, it contains much information on the Creeks, but, more important, Abel has recreated in exquisite detail the context for the Creek experience during the period.

The Union abandoned Indian Territory. The Confederacy made a major, and largely successful, effort to win its people to an alliance. Kenny A. Franks has recently published two excellent articles on Confederate Indian policy and administration in Indian Territory. His "An Analysis of the Confederate Treaties with the Five Civilized Tribes" [79] argues that Union abandonment, combined with a Southern origin and slavery, made alliance with the Confederacy a logical policy for all the Southern nations. Albert Pike, the Confederacy's commissioner to negotiate treaties of alliance, worked from June to October 1861 and obtained signed documents from all five. The Creeks signed first, the Cherokees last. The treaties, Franks shows, were similar and exceedingly generous. They guaranteed the territorial and political integrity of each nation, promised that none would ever be subject to the laws of any state or territory, recognized unrestricted self-government, and authorized the election of a delegate from each nation to the Confederate Congress. These and other benefits, Franks argues, made the Confederate treaties more liberal than any then in force with the United States. Assuming that pledges were honored, Southern victory would have secured virtual autonomy for the Southern nations. They would have received rights that in the United States were reserved for Whites only.

In "The Implementation of the Confederate Treaties with the Civilized Tribes" [80], Franks analyzes the administration of this policy. Franks gives Albert Pike credit for the generosity of the treaties and the Confederate Indian policy that was reflected in their provisions. Pike's good ideas were not enough, of course, and the press of the war delayed or prevented congressional action. As Franks points out, the Confederacy was poor, it was preoccupied, and Indian Territory was a long way from Richmond. The Confederacy broke its promises to the Creeks and to its other allies. The Confederacy, Franks concludes, probably promised more than it ever could have delivered.

Indian Territory was a bitter and bloody Civil War battleground. Dean Trickett published a series of articles on the subject under the general title, "The Civil War in the Indian Territory" [200]. Parts 3 and 4 of the series deal with the Creeks, who fought an exceptionally sharp series of skirmishes among themselves.

The lines of division within the Creek Nation are subject to some dispute. Daniel N. McIntosh, a son of William McIntosh, was the leading Confederate Creek. Opothle Yoholo, McIntosh's nemesis, was the leading Unionist. Trickett suggests that Opothle Yoholo was a Unionist because he hated the McIntoshes. Edwin C. Bearss, in "The Civil War Comes to Indian Territory, 1861: The Flight of Opothleyoholo" [17], argues that Opothle Yoholo, though not particularly pro-Union, feared McIntosh would kill him and fled in the only safe direction, north. As the owner of a large number of Black slaves, Opothle Yoholo could hardly be viewed as antislavery. LeRoy H. Fischer and Kenny A. Franks, in "Confederate Victory at Chusto-Talasah" [63], argue that the division was a continuation of the old Upper-Lower factionalism that had plagued the Creeks for generations, although in 1861 the personal animosity between the McIntoshes and Opothle Yoholo might have magnified the bitterness. These remarks do not exhaust the subject of Union versus Confederate Creek, but they at least suggest the nature of the debate.

The treaty of 10 June 1861 allied the Creek Nation to the Confederacy. Almost immediately, the pro-Confederate Creek leadership organized a cavalry unit. Most, if not all, of the Confederate Creeks were from

the Lower Towns. Opothle Yoholo, since Alabama days
the recognized leader of the Upper Creeks, opposed
involvement in the Civil War. His pleas for neutrality
ignored, he concluded that flight was preferable to vio-
lation of the treaties with the United States. Several
thousand Creeks accompanied Opothle Yoholo in the
evacuation to Kansas. Most were from the Upper
Towns, though not all, and a substantial number of the
Blacks of the Nation, both free and the slaves of fleeing
Creeks, joined. The movement began as a peaceful
withdrawal, with Opothle Yoholo and his followers car-
rying their possessions in an enormous wagon train
and driving thousands of head of cattle and horses.
The Confederate Creek Brigade gave chase, and during November and December 1861 the two groups
fought three battles. The last cost the (now) Unionist
Creeks all but the clothes on their backs. In a blinding
snowstorm and freezing temperatures they stumbled
into Kansas and the care of unprepared, disorganized,
penny-pinching, and callous federal officers who set
them up in disease-ridden refugee camps for the du-
ration of the war. In addition to the articles cited
above, interested students should consult two studies
written by Angie Debo: "The Site of the Battle of
Round Mountain, 1861" [53], and "The Location of
the Battle of Round Mountain" [55]. These articles are
far more informative than the titles suggest. Jerlena
King has published a useful short sketch, "Jackson
Lewis of the Confederate Creek Regiment" [110]. Dean
Banks, "Civil War Refugees from Indian Territory in

the North, 1861– 1864" [10], describes in shocking detail the deplorable conditions in Kansas. Most of these
refugees were Creeks, making this article much more
specifically Creek than is apparent in the title. Allen C.
Ashcraft, ed., "Confederate Indian Department Conditions in August, 1864" [7], is an edited reprint of a
report of Colonel R. W. Lee, Assistant Superintendent
of Indian Affairs, C.S.A., which indicates that pro-
South Indians also suffered in refugee camps. Though
their conditions were never so desperate as those in
Kansas, Confederate Creeks were ousted from their
Arkansas River valley plantations by the fighting and
had to make-do in huts on the Washita.

The Late Nineteenth Century

The United States Civil War did enormous social
and economic damage to the Creek Nation, and the
postwar years were literally ones of reconstruction. The
United States dealt badly with the nations of Indian
Territory. Forgetting that it had abandoned them in
1861, Congress passed a law in 1862 stipulating that
any native nation that had signed a treaty with the
Confederacy forfeited all rights to their annuities and
their lands. In 1865, when the war was over, the President notified the tribes that he did not want to impose
such harsh penalties and hoped they would reestablish
treaty relations with the United States. The new
treaties must abolish slavery, provide security for the

freedmen, and cede a large parcel of land for the relocation of other tribes in Indian Territory. From the Creeks the government demanded half their territory. The document made no distinction between the Union and Confederate Creeks, thus failing to recognize the sacrifices the loyal faction had made during the war. Rather, all Creeks were treated alike, as ex-Confederate enemies. As Gail Balman, "The Creek Treaty of 1866" [9], shows, this federal policy penalized the Unionists for their loyalty and excused the Confederates for their disloyalty.

The Unionist Creeks were angered by the treaty of 1866 and sought some adjustment of its provisions. Berlin B. Chapman, ed., "Unratified Treaty with the Creeks, 1868" [36], describes the efforts they made to modify the terms of the earlier agreement to increase the payment for the Creek cession and enlarge the compensation for destroyed property. The negotiations went far toward satisfying the loyal Creeks, but the treaty got lost in the shuffle of the late 1860s when the entire treaty system was under debate, and it was never ratified.

Ohland Morton, "Reconstruction in the Creek Nation" [135], and M. E. Thomas Bailey, *Reconstruction in Indian Territory: A Story of Avarice, Discrimination and Opportunism* [8], provide generalized interpretations of the late 1860s in the Creek Nation. Bailey's book, published in 1972, has a section on the Creeks. Both draw attention to the physical destruction of the Civil War and the massive rebuilding necessary to stimulate

economic recovery. Helga H. Harriman, "Economic
Conditions in the Creek Nation, 1865–1871" [92],
documents the recovery process. Harriman says there
was an economic revolution in the Creek Nation after
the war. Her proof is in production figures, livestock
census data, housing construction, and information on
road and river development. The extent to which these
statistics demonstrate revolutionary change is uncertain, however, since Harriman's prewar figures are in-
complete. Moreover, her interpretation is faulty. She
characterizes prewar Creeks as "wandering hunters"
who had been transformed during the late 1860s into
"peaceful farmers." Muriel H. Wright's "A Report to
the General Council of the Indian Territory Meeting at
Okmulgee in 1873" [214] is a useful supplement to
Harriman. The report of the Committee on Agriculture of an intertribal council that met during the early
1870s, it is a clear statement of the condition of agriculture in the Territory in 1873.

Aside from the tribal histories cited earlier, the
most elaborate analysis of Creek government was published in 1930 by Ohland Morton. Entitled "The Government of the Creek Indians" [134], it is an extensive
discussion of government structure, constitutionalism,
factionalism, and rebellion. There were four attempts
to overthrow the constitutional government between
1867 and 1901, each of which Morton explains as the
blind attempt of conservative Creeks "to return to the
primitive conditions of pre-removal." Despite this
rather narrow view of Creek political conflict, Morton's

study is a comprehensive overview that should be consulted early in any research project on the western period of Creek history.

There are few published accounts of the separate agencies and institutions of government in the Nation. No one has produced for the Creeks the kind of legal history that has been published in recent years on the Cherokees, for example. One brief article does exist, however, that should be mentioned. Carolyn Thomas Foreman's "The Light-Horse in the Indian Territory" [70], though not an ambitious analysis, does describe how this local police force worked and how it was used by tribal governments. Concerned with the institution territorywide, Foreman has a section on each Nation that cites the laws establishing and defining the light-horse.

There is much additional information on Creek politics and government affairs in a number of published biographical sketches. Samuel Checote is one of the best remembered postwar Creek leaders. O. A. Lambert, "Historical Sketch of Col. Samuel Checote, Once Chief of the Creek Nation" [113], and John Bartlett Meserve, "Chief Samuel Checote, with Sketches of Chiefs Locher Harjo and Ward Coachman" [131], describe a full-blood Lower Creek "progressive" who was a Methodist minister and an officer in the Confederate army before serving as principal chief of the Nation. Under the constitution of 1867, popular elections every four years chose a principal chief and a second chief. Checote was the first elected under the "reconstruction constitution." Oktarharsars Harjo, also called Sands, opposed Checote in the 1871 election and lost. Meserve, who has the Nation neatly divided into two categories — Lower Town, mixed-blood, "progressive," Confederate and Upper Town, full-blood, "conservative," Union — interprets the 1871 election as a progressive-conservative battle with Confederate-Unionist overtones. Disgusted by his defeat, Sands led a bloodless attack on the council at Okmulgee that quickly collapsed and achieved nothing. Checote, principal chief for twelve years, led the Creeks to what Lambert calls their "highest standard in moral and religious living."

Meserve also wrote accounts of "Chief Isparhecher" [127] and "The Perrymans" [130]. Isparhecher, conservative friend of Sands, led one of the revolts against constitutional government. Called the Green Peach War, it was a struggle between Isparhecher and Checote that lasted from 1880 to 1883. By 1882, Isparhecher had gathered about 350 warriors and threatened to close the council. Checote sent the national militia, under command of Pleasant Porter, to break up the camp of dissidents. They scattered, fled to the Kiowa country, and were captured by the United States Army, which took Isparhecher and his friends to Fort Gibson. The army released them in July 1883, after a settlement negotiated with the Checote government under federal supervision. Meserve's article on the Perryman family is confused by the large number of people dealt with and is therefore not very informative on specific matters. Indeed, all Meserve's writings need to be handled with care. His definition of the factional divisions in the Nation is so mechanistic that there is little room left for the unexpected. One should carefully compare Meserve's interpretations of the political events of the 1870s and 1880s with those of Debo in *The Road to Disappearance* [52].

Bert Hodges, "Notes on the History of the Creek Nation and Some of Its Leaders" [99], is really an extended biography of the very prominent McIntosh family. Joel D. Boyd, "Creek Indian Agents, 1834–1874" [23], covers the period in Indian Territory from the establishment of the first western Creek agency to the combination of agencies of all five southern nations into the Union Agency. There were fourteen agents in the forty years, notes Boyd in this collective biography—all good men with the best interests of the Creeks at heart.

The Creeks preferred to take care of themselves. Under the constitution of 1867 they established a popularly elected two-house National Council, with executive and judicial branches, and enacted a body of laws that were periodically published: in 1880 as *Constitution and Laws of the Muskogee Nation* [139]; in 1890, under the editorship of L. C. Perryman [156]; and in 1894 as W. A. Rentie, comp., *Acts and Resolutions of the National Council of the Muskogee Nation of 1893* [166]. Printed in both English and Muskogee, these volumes also contained decisions of the supreme court of the Muskogee Nation, the Creek treaties with the United

States, and the provisions of federal law that affected the Creeks. Alice M. Robertson, "The Creek Indian Council in Session" [167], describes the council and its style in 1878.

Education in the Creek Nation in the late nineteenth century was organized and supervised by the Council and its appointees, but mission groups continued to supply many teachers and some money. Debo, *The Road to Disappearance* [52], has the best summary of the history of education in the Nation. The more specialized studies are primarily biographies of individuals involved in Creek education, and they say little about the schools or the life of the students. Carolyn Thomas Foreman has two such articles: "Augusta Robertson Moore: A Sketch of Her Life and Times" [66], and "Israel G. Vore and Levering Manual Labor School" [68]. Like most of Carolyn Foreman's work, these are undocumented and largely anecdotal. Mrs. J. O. Misch's "Lilah D. Lindsey" [133] recounts the story of a Creek woman educated at Tullahassee and at colleges in Missouri and Ohio. The first Creek woman to receive the degree "Mistress of Arts," Lindsey returned to the Nation in the mid-1880s to teach at the Wealaka Mission boarding school. From then until her retirement from public affairs in the mid-1930s she was active in the educational and political life of the Creek Nation and Oklahoma. Joe C. Jackson, "Church School Education in the Creek Nation, 1898 to 1907" [108], describes Creek educational policy in the last years of the Nation, with special attention to the relationship between national officials and the mission groups.

As Creeks took over the educational institutions of the Nation, so they early assumed control of their Christian religious life. Native preachers led native congregations in Baptist and Methodist services conducted in native languages and adapted to conform to native social needs. Indeed, the rural church community came to be viewed by anthropologists as the basis of Creek cultural maintenance. Not much is known about those communities, but one 1970 article suggests that much information exists: Sharon A. Fife, "Baptist Indian Church: Thlewarle Mekko Sapkv Coko" [62], is a fascinating description of a neighborhood church and its people.

Students have access to several important reminiscences of life in the Creek Nation in the 1870s and 1880s. This material must be used with care, but such recollections of personal experiences provide extremely useful detailed historical information. Clarence W. Turner, "Events among the Muskogees during Sixty Years" [201], is the reminiscence of a trader at Okmulgee. Carolyn Thomas Foreman, ed., "Jeremiah Curtin in Indian Territory" [73] contains much information on Creek society and politics in the early 1880s. L. M. S. Wilson's "Reminiscences of Jim Tomm" [209] recalls the early experiences of a Creek freedman. And Eugene Current-Garcia, ed., with Dorothy B. Hatfield, *Shem, Ham and Japheth: The Papers of W. O. Tuggle* [48], is the reminiscence of a Georgia lawyer, employed by the Creeks to represent them in Washington, who was also an active amateur folklorist and student of Creek history.

The Allotment Crisis

The 1887 Dawes General Allotment Act specifically exempted from its application the "Five Civilized Tribes" of Indian Territory. These five nations held their lands under the removal treaties of the 1830s, reaffirmed by the reconstruction treaties of 1866, in fee-simple ownership. Congress could not, therefore, simply legislate their allotment. The laws of the United States protected the fee-simple land rights of even native nations. Congress believed in allotment, however, and took steps in the early 1890s to extend the policy. In 1893 Congress created the Dawes Commission to negotiate allotment with the Creeks and the other southern nations. It was necessary to get some form of agreement that could be considered a voluntary abandonment of fee-simple communal ownership. Through this and other acts Congress forced the Creeks to accept allotment, the destruction of their government, the eradication of their legal system, and the attempted elimination of their community life.

There is no history of Creek allotment, but Angie Debo's *And Still the Waters Run: The Betrayal of the Five Civilized Tribes* [51] is an outstanding general analysis of allotment in Indian Territory that contains a great deal of information on the Creeks. Many of the documents relating to the negotiations between the Creeks and the Dawes Commission are printed in *Acts and Resolutions of the National Council of the Muskogee Nation of 1893 and 1899, Inclusive* [140].

John Bartlett Meserve's "Chief Pleasant Porter" [126] is the biography of the principal chief between 1899 and 1907, the period when the final process of allotment was under way. As such, this is more than the personal interpretation of Porter; it is a reasonably thorough history of allotment policy and official Creek response.

There was much opposition to allotment among the Creek people, but none so vigorously presented as that under the leadership of Chitto Harjo, Crazy Snake. Born in 1854, Chitto Harjo participated in the conservative rebellions against constitutional government in the 1870s and 1880s and emerged in the 1890s as the spokesman of hostility to allotment and the Dawes Commission. In 1901, he attempted to establish a separate national government for the antiallotment Creeks. Organized at Hickory Ground, an Upper Creek town, this separatist council passed laws severely restricting the rights of Creeks to rent land to Whites or employ Whites on their property. With a body of light-horse to enforce their laws, the Hickory Ground government seemed to be armed and prepared to fight constitutional authority. The National Council mobilized the militia, arrested Chitto Harjo and his most prominent followers, and broke up the Hickory Ground government.

During the next several years Chitto Harjo remained a vociferous critic of allotment. In 1906, when a Senate committee came to Indian Territory to investigate the progress of allotment, Chitto Harjo delivered a stinging testimony, printed as John Bartlett Meserve, "The Plea of Crazy Snake (Chitto Harjo)" [129]. In it the old patriot argued the rights of the Creek people as guaranteed by a century of treaties with the United States. "All that I am begging of you, Honorable Senators," he concluded, "is that these ancient agreements and treaties wherein you promised to take care of me and my people, be fulfilled and that you will remove all the difficulties that have been raised in reference to my people and their country and I ask you to see that these promises are faithfully kept" (p. 908).

In 1908, Chitto Harjo and others reconstituted the Hickory Ground movement. The next year the gathering was again broken up, this time by a White sheriff's posse. Chitto Harjo escaped the manhunt, and the authorities never found him. Mace Davis, "Chitto Harjo" [50], and Mel H. Bolster, "The Smoked Meat Rebellion" [18], describe this conservative movement against allotment. Bolster says the final outburst, in 1909, was a race riot with Chitto Harjo's people the innocent victims. There was much talk, Bolster claims, of how dead Indians could not hold land claims.

Once under way, it was impossible to stop the allotment process. Even outspoken Indian opponents of the policy found that in the end they had to make peace with it and take whatever precautions they could to guard their rights as individuals in the new situation. Alexander Lawrence Posey, poet and editor of the Eufaula *Indian Journal,* was such a person. He blasted allotment in the pages of his paper, both in serious editorials and with the humorous "Fus Fixico Letters," but he also participated in an enrollment field party in 1905. Many people, isolated in the hills, conservative, unable to speak or read English, often unaware of their rights, failed to list their names on the Creek census. They had to be sought out to receive their allotments and be recorded on the tribal roll as citizens. As a man they could trust, Posey tried to help them get their tracts and to protect their interests. An important turn-of-the-century Creek man of letters, Posey left behind two journals that have been edited and published. Edward E. Dale, ed., "The Journal of Alexander Lawrence Posey, January 1 to September 4, 1897" [49], covers the period when he was superintendent of the Creek Orphanage. Posey's "Journal of Creek Enrollment Field Party 1905" [161], is an informative account of his efforts to convince conservatives to claim their allotments. Doris Challacombe, "Alexander Lawrence Posey" [34], and Leona G. Barnett, "Este Cate Emunkv (Red Man Always)" [11], are biographical sketches of Posey; Barnett's is especially valuable because it prints hard-to-find selections from the "Fus Fixico Letters."

The Creek National Council met for the last time in October 1905. It was a sad gathering that foreshadowed the end of the Creek Nation and the beginning of an uncertain time when the Creek people would be stripped of the institutional supports they had come to depend on and would have to learn new ways to confront the White world. Lonnie E. Underhill, "Hamlin Garland and the Final Council of the Creek Nation" [203], is a short and sensitive rendering of a segment of Garland's diary that recorded his visit to Okmulgee during the last days of the Council.

The Creeks in the Twentieth Century

Considering the impressive quantity and quality of the anthropological and historical material published about Creek life before 1900, it is surprising to discover how little has been done on the postallotment period. Even more striking, there seem to be few Swantons, Gatschets, or Debos preparing to carry on the tradition of first-class scholarship in Creek studies. Consequently, twentieth-century Creek ethnohistory is effectively unknown outside contemporary Creek society.

Angie Debo, *The Five Civilized Tribes of Oklahoma: Report on Social and Economic Conditions* [54], a commissioned study for the Indian Rights Association completed in 1951, is both short and general. Debo notes that, unlike the Cherokees and Choctaws, the Creeks received their allotments in unified 160-acre parcels, most of which could reasonably support a single family. This, plus the vitality of Creek communities and the maintenance of the town organization in an unofficial setting, left the Creeks in a relatively strong social and economic position.

Alexander Spoehr's "Changing Kinship Systems" [181] and Morris E. Opler's "The Creek 'Town'" [146], both previously cited, support Debo's contention. Despite allotment, Creek people have maintained their loyalty to their ancient towns, a large number of which continue to function as social, ceremonial , and political units. Along with the neighborhood churches and the many stomp grounds, they continue to provide the Creeks with a strong sense of community. These institutions have also encouraged the retention, perhaps more persistently than among any other allotted people in Oklahoma, of their native languages. Indeed, some scholars believe the Creeks enjoy one of the most traditional native societies in the United States.

Students can find additional information on the Oklahoma Creeks in the twentieth century in the previously cited works by Donald Green [84] and Muriel Wright [213].

The small Creek community in southern Alabama is even less well known. Frank G. Speck, on his way to Louisiana in 1941 on a Bureau of Indian Affairs mission, "discovered" them in an obscure settlement near Pensacola, Florida. In two short articles, "Notes on Social and Economic Conditions among the Creek Indians of Alabama in 1941" [178] and "The Road to Disappearance: Creek Indians Surviving in Alabama, a Mixed Culture Community" [179], Speck briefly describes a "remnant society" that, he argues, has lost most of its identity as Creek. It should come as no surprise to scholars, however, that this "vanishing community," like so many others, has refused to evaporate. On the contrary, as J. Anthony Paredes, "The Emergence of Contemporary Eastern Creek Indian Identity" [154] shows, during the last quarter-century the Creeks of Poarch, Escambia County, Alabama, have experienced a social and cultural revitalization of significant proportions. The work of Paredes, along with the 1977 prize-winning essay, "Instant Indians: An Analysis of Cultural Identity in the American South" [204], by Amelia Walker, a graduate student at the University of Chicago, points to the irony of current Creek studies. The "lost" Creeks in Alabama are receiving more scholarly attention than the people of the Creek Nation in Oklahoma. Walker is preparing a full-length study of the present population of the Creeks in Oklahoma, which promises to fill a large gap in our knowledge of contemporary Creeks.

ALPHABETICAL LIST AND INDEX

*Denotes items suitable for secondary school students

[4]   ———. 1925. *The American Indian under Reconstruction.* Vol. 3 of *The Slaveholding Indians.* Cleveland: Arthur H. Clark.   (53)

[5]   Adair, James. 1775. *The History of the American Indians: Particularly Those Adjoining to the Mississippi, East and West Florida, Georgia, South and North Carolina and Virginia.* London: E. C. Dilly. Reprinted, Johnson City, Tenn.: Watauga Press, 1930.   (vii, 15)

[6]   Alden, John Richard. 1944. *John Stuart and the Southern Colonial Frontier: A Study of Indian Relations, War, Trade and Land Problems in the Southern Wilderness, 1754–1775.* London: Oxford University Press; Ann Arbor: University of Michigan Press.   (28)

[7]   Ashcraft, Allen C., ed. 1963. "Confederate Indian Department Conditions in August, 1864." *Chronicles of Oklahoma* 41:270–85.   (57)

[8]   Bailey, Minnie Elizabeth Thomas. 1972. *Reconstruction in Indian Territory: A Story of Avarice, Discrimination and Oppor-*

tunism. Port Washington, N.Y.: Kennikat Press. (58)

[9] Balman, Gail. 1970. "The Creek Treaty of 1866." *Chronicles of Oklahoma* 48:184–96. (58)

[10] Banks, Dean. 1963. "Civil War Refugees from Indian Territory in the North, 1861–1864." *Chronicles of Oklahoma* 41:286–98. (57)

[11] Barnett, Leona G. 1968. "Este Cate Emunkv (Red Man Always)." *Chronicles of Oklahoma* 46:20–40. (68)

[12] Bartram, John. 1942. "Diary of a Journey through the Carolinas, Georgia, and Florida from July 1, 1765, to April 10, 1766." Francis Harper, ed. *Transactions of the American Philosophical Society,* n.s., 33, part 1:1–120. (22)

[13] Bartram, William. 1773–74. "Travels in Georgia and Florida, 1773–74: A Report to Doctor John Fothergill." In *Transactions of the American Philosophical Society,* n.s. 33, part 2 (1943): 121–242. (22)

[14]   ———. 1789. "Observations on the Creek and Cherokee Indians," with prefatory and supplementary notes by E. G. Squier. In *Transactions of the American Ethnological Society* 3, part 1: 1–81 (1853). New York: American Ethnological Society.   (22)

[15]   ———. 1791. *Travels through North and South Carolina, Georgia, East and West Florida, the Cherokee Country, the Extensive Territories of the Muscogulges or Creek Confederacy, and the Country of the Choctaws. Containing an Account of the Soil and Natural Productions of Those Regions; Together with Observations on the Manners of the Indians.* Philadelphia: James and Johnson. Reprinted as *Travels of William Bartram,* ed. Mark Van Doren, New York: Dover 1928. New ed. in facsimile, New York: Barnes and Noble, 1940. New ed., ed. Francis Harper, New Haven, Yale University Press, 1958.   (23)

[16]   Bast, Homer. 1949. "Creek Indian Affairs, 1775–1778." *Georgia Historical Quarterly* 33:1–25.   (27)

[17] Bearss, Edwin C. 1972. "The Civil War
Comes to Indian Territory, 1861: The
Flight of Opothleyoholo." *Journal of the
West* 1:9–42.   (55)

[18] Bolster, Mel H. 1953. "The Smoked
Meat Rebellion." *Chronicles of Oklahoma*
31:37–55.   (67)

[19] Bolton, Herbert E. 1925. "Spanish Re-
sistance to the Carolina Traders in
Western Georgia (1680–1704)." *Georgia
Historical Quarterly* 9:115–30.   (21)

[20] Bonner, James C. 1957. "Tustunugee
Hutkee and Creek Factionalism on the
Georgia-Alabama Frontier." *Alabama
Review* 10:111–25.   (42)

[21] ———. 1958. "William McIntosh." In
*Georgians in Profile: Historical Essays in
Honor of Ellis Merton Coulter,* ed. Horace
Montgomery, pp. 114–43. Athens:
University of Georgia Press.   (42)

[22] ———, ed. 1960. "Journal of a Mission
to Georgia in 1827." *Georgia Historical
Quarterly* 44:74–85.   (44)

[23]   Boyd, Joel D. 1973. "Creek Indian Agents, 1834–1874." *Chronicles of Oklahoma* 51:37–58.   (62)

[24]   Brannon, Peter A. 1920. "Aboriginal Towns in Alabama." In *Handbook of the Alabama Anthropological Society,* pp. 42–58. Montgomery, Ala.: Brown Printing Company.   (18)

[25]   ———, ed. 1924. "Journal of James A. Tait for the Year 1813." *Georgia Historical Quarterly* 8:229–39.   (39)

[26]   ———. 1935. *The Southern Indian Trade: Being Particularly a Study of Material from the Tallapoosa River Valley of Alabama.* Montgomery, Ala.: Paragon Press.   (5)

[27]   ———. 1951. "Creek Indian War, 1836–37." *Alabama Historical Quarterly* 13:156–58.   (46)

[28]   ———. 1952. "Pensacola Indian Trade." *Florida Historical Quarterly* 31:1–15.   (5)

[29] Buckner, Henry Frieland. 1860. *A Grammar of the Maskwke or Creek Language.* G. Herrod, interp. Marion, Ala.: Domestic and Indian Mission Board of the Southern Baptist Convention. (7)

[30] Campbell, John Archibald. 1899. "The Creek War of 1836." *Transactions of the Alabama Historical Society* 3:162–66. (46)

[31] Campbell, Thomas. 1930. "Thomas Campbell to Lord Deane Gordon: An Account of the Creek Nation, 1764." *Florida Historical Quarterly* 8:156–64. (27)

[32] Caughey, John W. 1932. "Alexander McGillivray and the Creek Crisis in 1783–84." In *New Spain and the Anglo-American West: Historical Contributions Presented to Herbert Eugene Bolton,* ed. Charles W. Hackett, George P. Hammond, and J. Lloyd Mecham, 1:263–88. Lancaster, Pa.: Lancaster Press. Reprinted, New York: Kraus, 1969. (30)

[33] ———. 1938. *McGillivray of the Creeks.*

Norman: University of Oklahoma
Press. Reprinted, 1959.   (30)

[34] Challacombe, Doris. 1933. "Alexander
      Lawrence Posey." *Chronicles of Oklahoma*
      11:1011–18.   (68)

[35] Chambers, Nella J. 1959. "The Creek
      Indian Factory at Fort Mitchell." *Ala-
      bama Historical Quarterly* 21:15–53. (36)

[36] Chapman, Berlin B., ed. 1938. "Unrat-
      ified Treaty with the Creeks, 1868."
      Chronicles of Oklahoma 16:337–45.   (58)

[37] Coley, C. J. 1958. "Creek Treaties,
      1790–1832." *Alabama Review* 11:163–
      76.   (19)

[38] Corbitt, D. C., trans. and ed. 1936–41.
      "Papers Relating to the Georgia-Florida
      Frontier, 1784–1800." *Georgia Historical
      Quarterly* 20:356–65; 21:73–83, 185–
      88, 274–93, 373–81; 22:72–6, 184–
      91, 286–91, 391–94; 23:77–9, 189–
      202, 300–03, 381–87; 24:77–83,
      150–57, 257–71, 374–81; 25:67–76,
      159–71.   (30)

[39]* Corkran, David H. 1967. *The Creek Frontier, 1540–1783*. Norman: University of Oklahoma Press. (21, 26, 28)

[40] Corry, John Pitts. 1936. *Indian Affairs in Georgia, 1732–1756*. Philadelphia: George S. Ferguson. (25)

[41] ———. 1941. "Some New Light on the Bosomworth Claims." *Georgia Historical Quarterly* 25:195–224. (25)

[42]* Cotterill, Robert Spencer. 1954. *The Southern Indians: The Story of the Civilized Tribes before Removal*. Norman: University of Oklahoma Press. (19)

[43] Coulter, E. Merton. 1927. "Mary Musgrove, 'Queen of the Creeks': A Chapter of Early Georgia Troubles." *Georgia Historical Quarterly* 11:1–30. (24)

[44] Covington, James W. 1968. "Migration of the Seminoles into Florida, 1700–1820." *Florida Historical Quarterly* 46:340–57. (viii)

[45]   Crane, Verner Winslow. 1918. "The
        Origin of the Name of the Creek Indi-
        ans." *Journal of American History*
        5:339–42.   (7)

[46]*   ———. 1928. *The Southern Frontier,*
        1670–1732. Durham, N.C.: Duke Uni-
        versity Press; Ann Arbor: University of
        Michigan Press, 1929.   (21)

[47]   ———. 1930. "The Origins of Geor-
        gia." *Georgia Historical Quarterly* 14:93–
        110.   (24)

[48]   Current-Garcia, Eugene, ed., with
        Dorothy B. Hatfield. 1973. *Shem, Ham*
        and Japheth: The Papers of W. O. Tuggle
        Comprising His Indian Diary, Sketches and
        Observations, Myths and Washington Jour-
        nal in the Territory and at the Capital,
        1879–1882. Athens, Ga.: University of
        Georgia Press.   (64)

[49]   Dale, Edward Everett, ed. 1967–68.
        "The Journal of Alexander Lawrence
        Posey, January 1 to September 4,
        1897." *Chronicles of Oklahoma* 54:393–
        432.   (68)

[50] Davis, Mace. 1935. "Chitto Harjo."
Chronicles of Oklahoma 13:139–45. (67)

[51]* Debo, Angie. 1940. *And Still the Waters
Run: The Betrayal of the Five Civilized
Tribes.* Princeton: Princeton University
Press. Reprinted, 1972. (65)

[52]* ———. 1941. *The Road to Disappearance.* Norman: University of Oklahoma
Press. New ed., 1967. (16, 62, 63)

[53] ———. 1949. "The Site of the Battle
of Round Mountain, 1861." *Chronicles of
Oklahoma* 27:187–206. (56)

[54] ———. 1951. *The Five Civilized Tribes
of Oklahoma: Report on Social and Economic Conditions.* Philadelphia: Indian
Rights Association. (69)

[55] ———. 1963. "The Location of the
Battle of Round Mountain." *Chronicles
of Oklahoma* 41:70–104. (56)

[56] DeVorsey, Louis, Jr. 1970. "Indian
Boundaries in Colonial Georgia." *Georgia Historical Quarterly* 54:63–78. (27)

[57]   Doster, James Fletcher. 1974. *The Creek Indians and Their Florida Lands, 1740–1823.* 2 vols. United States Indian Claims Commission, American Indian Ethnohistory Series. New York: Garland.   (23, 39)

[58]   Downes, Randolph C. 1937. "Creek-American Relations, 1782–1790." *Georgia Historical Quarterly* 21:142–84.   (31)

[59]   ———. 1942. "Creek-American Relations, 1790–1795." *Journal of Southern History* 8:350–73.   (32)

[60]   DuChateau, André Paul. 1974. "The Creek Nation on the Eve of Civil War." *Chronicles of Oklahoma* 52:290–315.   (52)

[61]   Fairbanks, Charles H. 1952. "Creek and Pre-Creek." In *Archeology of the Eastern United States,* ed. James B. Griffin, pp. 285–300. Chicago: University of Chicago Press.   (4)

[62]   Fife, Sharon A. 1970. "Baptist Indian Church: Thlewarle Mekko Sapkv Coko." *Chronicles of Oklahoma* 48:451–66.   (64)

[63]   Fischer, LeRoy H., and Kenny A. Franks. 1971–72. "Confederate Victory at Chusto-Talasah." *Chronicles of Oklahoma* 49:452–76.   (55)

[64]   Floyd, John. 1949. "Letters of John Floyd, 1813–1838." *Georgia Historical Quarterly* 33:228–69.   (39)

[65]   Fogelson, Raymond D., ed. Forthcoming. *The Southeast.* Vol. 14 of *The Handbook of North American Indians,* gen. ed., William G. Sturtevant. 20 vols. Washington, D.C.: Government Printing Office for the Smithsonian Institution.   (14)

[66]   Foreman, Carolyn Thomas. 1935. "Augusta Robertson Moore: A Sketch of Her Life and Times." *Chronicles of Oklahoma* 13:399–420.   (63)

[67]   ———. 1943. "A Creek Pioneer: Notes Concerning 'Aunt Sue' Rogers and Her Family." *Chronicles of Oklahoma* 21:271–79.   (52)

[68]   ———. 1947. "Israel G. Vore and Levering Manual Labor School." *Chronicles of Oklahoma* 25:198–217.   (63)

[69]   ———. 1948. "Report of the Reverend R. M. Loughridge to the Board of
Foreign Missions Regarding the Creek
Mission." *Chronicles of Oklahoma*
26:278–84.   (51)

[70]   ———. 1956. "The Light-Horse in the
Indian Territory." *Chronicles of Oklahoma*
34:17–43.   (60)

[71]   ———. 1960. "The White Lieutenant
and Some of His Contemporaries."
Chronicles of Oklahoma 38:425–40.   (33)

[72]   ———. 1964. "Lee Compere and the
Creek Indians." *Chronicles of Oklahoma*
42:291–99.   (50)

[73]   ———, ed. 1948. "Jeremiah Curtin in
Indian Territory." *Chronicles of Oklahoma*
26:345–56.   (64)

[74]*   Foreman, Grant. 1930. *Indians and
Pioneers: The Story of the American South-
west before 1830.* New Haven: Yale Uni-
versity Press; London: H. Milford,
Oxford University Press. New ed.,
Norman: University of Oklahoma
Press, 1936.   (47)

[75]* ———. 1932. *Indian Removal: The Emigration of the Five Civilized Tribes of Indians.* Norman: University of Oklahoma Press. New ed., 1953. Reprinted, 1976. (48)

[76]* ———. 1933. *Advancing the Frontier, 1830–1860.* Norman: University of Oklahoma Press. Reprinted, 1968. (50)

[77]* ———. 1934. *The Five Civilized Tribes: Cherokee, Chickasaw, Choctaw, Creek, Seminole.* Intro. by John R. Swanton. Norman: University of Oklahoma Press. Reprinted, 1974. (48)

[78] ———, ed. 1930. *A Traveler in Indian Territory; The Journal of Ethan Allen Hitchcock, Late Major-General in the United States Army.* Cedar Rapids, Iowa: Torch Press. (49)

[79] Franks, Kenny A. 1972–73. "An Analysis of the Confederate Treaties with the Five Civilized Tribes." *Chronicles of Oklahoma* 50:458–73. (53)

[80] ———. 1973. "The Implementation of the Confederate Treaties with the Civilized Tribes." *Chronicles of Oklahoma* 51:21–34. (54)

[81]   Gatschet, Albert S. 1884–88. *A Migration Legend of the Creek Indians, with a
Linguistic, History and Ethnographic Introduction.* Philadelphia: Daniel G.
Brinton.   (7)

[82]   ——. 1888. "Tchikilli's Kasi'hta
Legend in the Creek and Hitchiti Languages with a Critical Commentary and
Full Glossaries to Both Texts." *Transactions of the Academy of Science of St. Louis*
5:33–239.   (9)

[83]   ——. 1901. "Towns and Villages of
the Creek Confederacy in the XVIII
and XIX Centuries." *Report of the Alabama History Commission* 1:386–415.   (18)

[84]*   Green, Donald E. 1973. *The Creek
People.* Phoenix: Indian Tribal Series. (17, 70)

[85]   Green, Michael D. 1973. "Federal-State
Conflict in the Administration of Indian Policy: Georgia, Alabama, and the
Creeks, 1824–1834." Ph.D. diss., University of Iowa.   (45)

[86]   ———. Forthcoming. "Alexander McGillivray." In *Perspectives on American Indian Leadership*, ed. R. David Edmunds. Lincoln: University of Nebraska Press.   (32)

[87]   Haas, Mary R. 1940. "Creek Inter-town Relations." *American Anthropologist* 42:479–89.   (11)

[88]   ———. 1971. "Southeastern Indian Linguistics." In *Red, White and Black: Symposium on Indians in the Old South*, ed. Charles Hudson, pp. 44–54. Athens: University of Georgia Press.   (6)

[89]   Halbert, Henry Sale, and T. H. Ball. 1895. *The Creek War of 1813 and 1814.* Chicago: Donohue and Henneberry. Reprinted, with introduction and annotations by Frank L. Owsley, Jr. University, Ala.: University of Alabama Press, 1969.   (40)

[90]   Hall, Arthur H. 1934. "The Red Stick War: Creek Indian Affairs during the War of 1812." *Chronicles of Oklahoma* 12:264–93.   (40)

[91]   Hally, David J. 1971. "The Archaeology
of European-Indian Contact in the
Southeast." In *Red, White and Black:
Symposium on Indians in the Old South,* ed.
Charles Hudson, pp. 55–66. Athens:
University of Georgia Press.   (5)

[92]   Harriman, Helga H. 1973. "Economic
Conditions in the Creek Nation,
1865–1871." *Chronicles of Oklahoma*
51:325–35.   (59)

[93]   Hassig, Ross. 1974. "Internal Conflict
in the Creek War of 1813–1814."
Ethnohistory 21:251–71.   (40)

[94]   Hawkins, Benjamin. 1848. *A Sketch of
the Creek Country in the Years 1798 and
1799. Collections of the Georgia Historical
Society* 3, part 1. Reprinted, New York:
Kraus, 1971.   (36)

[95]   ———. 1916. *Letters of Benjamin Hawkins, 1796–1806. Collections of the Georgia Historical Society* 9.   (36)

[96]   Hewitt, J. N. B. 1939. *Notes on the Creek
Indians,* ed. John R. Swanton. United

States Bureau of American Ethnology Bulletin 123:119–59. Washington, D.C.: Government Printing Office.   (14)

[97]   Hinds, Roland. 1939. "Early Creek Missions." *Chronicles of Oklahoma* 17:48–61.   (51)

[98]   Hodge, Frederick Webb, ed. 1907–10. *Handbook of American Indians North of Mexico.* 2 vols. United States Bureau of American Ethnology Bulletin 30. Washington, D.C.: Government Printing Office. Reprinted, New York: Pageant Books, 1959; Totowa, N.J.: Rowman and Littlefield, 1975.   (18)

[99]   Hodges, Bert. 1965. "Notes on the History of the Creek Nation and Some of Its Leaders." *Chronicles of Oklahoma* 43:9–18.   (62)

[100]   Holland, James W. 1968. "Andrew Jackson and the Creek War: Victory at the Horseshoe." *Alabama Review* 21:243–75.   (39)

[101]   Holmes, Jack D. L. 1969. "Spanish Treaties with the West Florida Indians,

1784–1802." *Florida Historical Quarterly* 48:140–54.   (31)

[102]   Hryniewicki, Richard J. 1964. "The Creek Treaty of Washington, 1826." *Georgia Historical Quarterly* 48:425–41.   (43)

[103]   ———. 1968. "The Creek Treaty of November 15, 1827." *Georgia Historical Quarterly* 52:1–15.   (43)

[104]* Hudson, Charles M. 1976. *The Southeastern Indians.* Knoxville: University of Tennessee Press.   (1, 14)

[105]   Innerarity, John. 1930. "The Creek Nation, Debtor to John Forbes and Company, Successors to Panton, Leslie and Company. A Journal of John Innerarity, 1812." *Florida Historical Quarterly* 9:67–89.   (37)

[106]   ———. 1940. "A Prelude to the Creek War of 1813–1814," ed. Elizabeth Howard West. *Florida Historical Quarterly* 18:247–66.   (38)

[107]   Jack, Theodore H. 1916. "Alabama and the Federal Government: The Creek Indian Controversy." *Journal of American History* 3:301–17.   (44)

[108]   Jackson, Joe C. 1968. "Church School Education in the Creek Nation, 1898 to 1907." *Chronicles of Oklahoma* 46:312–30.   (63)

[109]   Kappler, Charles J., comp. 1903–41. *Indian Affairs, Laws and Treaties.* 5 vols. Washington, D.C.: Government Printing Office. Vol. 2. *Treaties,* 1904. Senate Document no. 319, 59th Congress, 2d sess., serial no. 4624. Reprinted, New York: Interland, 1972.   (19)

[110]   King, Jerlena. 1963. "Jackson Lewis of the Confederate Creek Regiment." *Chronicles of Oklahoma* 41:66–69.   (56)

[111]   Kinnaird, Lawrence. 1931. "International Rivalry in Creek Country, Part 1: The Ascendency of Alexander McGillivray, 1783–1789." *Florida Historical Quarterly* 10:59–85.   (31)

[112]   Kinnaird, Lucia Burk. 1932. "The Rock Landing Conference of 1789." *North Carolina Historical Review* 9:349–65.   (32)

[113]   Lambert, O. A. 1926. "Historical Sketch of Col. Samuel Checote, Once Chief of the Creek Nation." *Chronicles of Oklahoma* 4:275–80.   (60)

[114]   Lauderdale, Virginia E. 1948. "Tullahassee Mission." *Chronicles of Oklahoma* 26:285–300.   (51)

[115]*   Lewis, Thomas McDowell Nelson, and Madeline Kneberg. 1958. *Tribes That Slumber: Indian Times in the Tennessee Region.* Knoxville: University of Tennessee Press.   (2)

[116]   Logsdon, Guy. 1976. "Oklahoma's First Book: 'Istutsi in Naktsoku,' by John Fleming." *Chronicles of Oklahoma* 54:179–91.   (51)

[117]   Loomis, Augustus W. 1968. "Scenes in the Indian Territory: Kowetah Mission." *Chronicles of Oklahoma* 46:64–72.   (51)

[118] Loughridge, Robert M., and David M.
       Hodge. 1890. *English and Muskogee Dic-*
       tionary. St. Louis: J. T. Smith.   (7)

[119] McCorvey, Thomas C. 1904. "The
       Mission of Francis Scott Key to Ala-
       bama in 1833." *Transactions of the Ala-*
       bama Historical Society 4:141–65.   (44)

[120] McKenney, Thomas L. 1846. *Memoirs,*
       Official and Personal: With Sketches of
       Travels among the Northern and Southern
       Indians. New York: Paine and Burgess.
       Reprinted, Lincoln: University of Ne-
       braska Press, 1973.   (44)

[121] McKenney Thomas L., and James T.
       Hall. 1838–44. *History of the Indian*
       Tribes of North America, with Biographical
       Sketches and Anecdotes of the Principal
       Chiefs, Embellished with One Hundred and
       Twenty Portraits from the Indian Gallery in
       the Department of War, at Washington. 3
       vols. Philadelphia: Frederick W.
       Greenough. New ed., ed. Frederick W.
       Hodge, Edinburgh: J. Grant, 1933–34.   (19)

[122] Mason, Carol I. 1963. "Eighteenth Cen-

tury Culture Change among the Lower Creeks." *Florida Anthropologist* 16:65–80.   (4)

[123]   Mattison, Ray H. 1946. "The Creek Trading House—From Coleraine to Fort Hawkins." *Georgia Historical Quarterly* 30:169–84.   (36)

[124]   Mereness, Newton Dennison. 1916. *Travels in the American Colonies.* New York: Macmillan.   (26)

[125]   Meserve, John Bartlett. 1931. "Chief Opothleyahola." *Chronicles of Oklahoma* 9:439–53.   (52)

[126]   ———. 1931. "Chief Pleasant Porter." *Chronicles of Oklahoma* 9:318–34.   (66)

[127]   ———. 1932. "Chief Isparhecher." *Chronicles of Oklahoma* 10:52–76.   (61)

[128]   ———. 1932. "The MacIntoshes." *Chronicles of Oklahoma* 10:310–25.   (52)

[129]   ———. 1933. "The Plea of Crazy Snake (Chitto Harjo)." *Chronicles of Oklahoma* 11:899–911.   (67)

[130]   ———. 1937. "The Perrymans." *Chronicles of Oklahoma* 15:166–84.   (61)

[131]   ———. 1938. "Chief Samuel Checote, with Sketches of Chiefs Locher Harjo and Ward Coachman." *Chronicles of Oklahoma* 16:401–9.   (60)

[132]   Milfort, Louis LeClerc. 1956. *Memoirs; or, A Cursory Glance at My Different Travels and My Sojourn in the Creek Nation,* ed. John Francis McDermott, trans. Geraldine de Courcy. Originally published in French, 1802. Chicago: R. R. Donnelley. New ed., trans. and ed. Ben C. McCary, Savannah, Ga.: Beehive Press, 1972.   (15)

[133]   Misch, Mrs. J. O. 1955. "Lilah D. Lindsey." *Chronicles of Oklahoma* 33:193–201.   (63)

[134]   Morton, Ohland. 1930. "The Govern-

ment of the Creek Indians." *Chronicles of Oklahoma* 8:42–64, 189–225. (59)

[135]   ———. 1931. "Reconstruction in the Creek Nation." *Chronicles of Oklahoma* 9:171–79. (58)

[136]*   Muller, Jon D. 1978. "The Southeast." In *Ancient Native Americans,* ed. Jesse D. Jennings, pp. 281–325. San Francisco: W. H. Freeman. (1)

[137]   Murdock, George Peter, and Timothy J. O'Leary. 1975. *Ethnographic Bibliography of North America.* 5 vols. 4th ed. New Haven: Human Relations Area Files Press. (16)

[138]   Murdock, Richard K., ed. 1956. "Mission to the Creek Nation in 1794." *Florida Historical Quarterly* 34:266–84. (34)

[139]   Muskogee Nation. 1880. *Constitution and Laws of the Muskogee Nation.* Saint Louis: Levison and Blythe Stationery Company. Reprinted, Wilmington: Scholarly Resources, 1975. (62)

[140] ———. 1900. *Acts and Resolutions of the National Council of the Muskogee Nation of 1893 and 1899, Inclusive.* Muskogee: Phoenix Printing Company. Reprinted, Wilmington: Scholarly Resources, 1975. (66)

[141] Nichols, Frances Sellman. 1954. *Index to Schoolcraft's Indian Tribes of the United States.* United States Bureau of American Ethnology Bulletin 152. Washington, D.C.: Government Printing Office. (16)

[142] Nuñez, Theron A., Jr. 1958. "Creek Nativism and the Creek War of 1813–1814." *Ethnohistory* 5:1–47, 131–75, 292–301. (37)

[143] O'Donnell, James H., III. 1965. "Alexander McGillivray: Training for Leadership, 1777–1783." *Georgia Historical Quarterly* 49:172–86. (28)

[144] ———. 1973. *Southern Indians in the American Revolution.* Knoxville: University of Tennessee Press. (28)

[145] "Oglethorpe's Treaty with the Lower

Creek Indians." 1920. *Georgia Historical Quarterly* 4:3–16.   (24)

[146] Opler, Morris E. 1952. "The Creek 'Town' and the Problem of Creek Indian Political Reorganization." In *Human Problems in Technological Change,* ed., Edward H. Spicer, pp. 165–80. New York: Russell Sage Foundation. (10, 70)

[147]* Orrmont, Arthur. 1967. *Diplomat in Warpaint: Chief Alexander McGillivray of the Creeks.* London: Abelard-Schuman.   (31)

[148] Owen, Marie Bankhead. 1950. "Indians in Alabama." *Alabama Historical Quarterly* 12:5–91.   (18)

[149] Owen, Thomas M. 1950. "Indian Tribes and Towns in Alabama." *Alabama Historical Quarterly* 12:118–241.   (18)

[150] ———. 1951. "Alabama Indian Chiefs." *Alabama Historical Quarterly* 13:5–91.   (18)

[151] Owsley, Frank L., Jr. 1968. "Benjamin

Hawkins: The First Modern Indian Agent." *Alabama Historical Quarterly* 30:7–13. (35)

[152] ———. 1970. "Francis Scott Key's Mission to Alabama in 1833." *Alabama Review* 32:181–92. (45)

[153] ———. 1971. "The Fort Mims Massacre." *Alabama Review* 24:192–204. (39)

[154] Parades, J. Anthony. 1974. "The Emergence of Contemporary Eastern Creek Indian Identity." In *Social and Cultural Identity: Problems of Persistence and Change,* ed. Thomas K. Fitzgerald. Athens: University of Georgia Press. (71)

[155] Pennington, Edgar Legare, ed. 1931. "Some Ancient Georgia Indian Lore." *Georgia Historical Quarterly* 15:192–98. (8)

[156] Perryman, L. C. 1890. *Constitution and Laws of the Muskogee Nation.* Muskogee: Phoenix Printing Company. Reprinted, Wilmington: Scholarly Resources, 1975. (62)

[157]   Phillips, Ulrich Bonnell. 1902. *Georgia and States Rights: A Study of the Political History of Georgia from the Revolution to the Civil War, with Particular Regard to Federal Relations.* In Annual Report of the American Historical Association for 1901, vol. 2:3–224. Washington: Government Printing Office. New ed., Louis Filler, ed., Yellow Springs, Ohio: Antioch Press, 1968.   (43)

[158]   Pickett, Albert James. 1851. *History of Alabama, and Incidentally of Georgia and Mississippi, from the Earliest Period.* 2 vols. Charleston: Walker and James. New eds., Sheffield, Alabama: R. C. Randolph, 1896; Birmingham, Alabama: Webb Book Company, 1900. Reprint of 1900 ed. available, Tuscaloosa, Ala.: Willo Publishing Company, 1962; Spartanburg, S.C.: Reprint Company, 1975.   (23)

[159]   Pilling, James Constantine. 1889. *Bibliography of the Muskhogean Languages.* United States Bureau of American Ethnology Bulletin 9. Washington, D.C.: Government Printing Office. Reprinted, New York: AMS, 1973.   (7)

[160]   Pope, John A. 1792. *A Tour through the Southern and Western Territories of the United States of North-America; the Spanish Dominions on the River Mississippi, and the Floridas; the Countries of the Creek Nations; and Many Uninhabited Parts.* Richmond, Va.: John Dixon. New ed., New York: C. L. Woodward, 1888. Reprint of original ed., New York: Arno, 1971; Gainesville: University Presses of Florida, 1979.   (33)

[161]   Posey, Alexander. 1968. "Journal of Creek Enrollment Field Party 1905." *Chronicles of Oklahoma* 46:2–19.   (68)

[162]   Pound, Merritt Bloodworth. 1929. "Benjamin Hawkins, Indian Agent." *Georgia Historical Quarterly* 13:392–409.   (35)

[163]   ———. 1951. *Benjamin Hawkins, Indian Agent.* Athens: University of Georgia Press.   (35)

[164]   ———. 1958. "Benjamin Hawkins." In *Georgians in Profile: Historical Essays in Honor of Ellis Merton Coulter,* ed. Horace Montgomery, pp. 89–113. Athens: University of Georgia Press.   (35)

[165]* Prucha, Francis Paul, S.J. 1977. *A Bibliographical Guide to the History of Indian-White Relations in the United States.* Chicago: University of Chicago Press for the Center for the History of the American Indian, Newberry Library.   (ix)

[166] Rentie, W. A., comp. 1894. *Acts and Resolutions of the National Council of the Muskogee Nation of 1893.* Muskogee: Phoenix Printing Company. Reprinted, Wilmington: Scholarly Resources, 1975.   (62)

[167] Robertson, Alice M. 1933. "The Creek Indian Council in Session." *Chronicles of Oklahoma* 11:895–98.   (63)

[168] Ross, Daniel J. J., and Bruce S. Chappell, eds. 1976. "Visit to the Indian Nations: The Diary of John Hambly." *Florida Historical Quarterly* 55:60–73.   (34)

[169] Sapulpa, William A. 1926. "Sapulpa." *Chronicles of Oklahoma* 4:329–32.   (52)

[170] Savage, William W., Jr. 1976. "Creek Colonization in Oklahoma." *Chronicles of Oklahoma* 54:34–43.   (48)

[171] Schoolcraft, Henry Rowe. 1851–57. *Historical and Statistical Information Respecting the History, Condition, and Prospects of the Indian Tribes of the United States.* 6 vols. Illustrated by Seth Eastman. Philadelphia: Lippincott, Grambo. Reprinted, New York: Paladin Press, 1969; New York: AMS, 1977. See [141] for index. (15)

[172] Sears, William H. 1955. "Creek and Cherokee Culture in the Eighteenth Century." *American Antiquity* 21:143–49. (3)

[173] Smith, Buckingham, trans. 1866. *Narratives of the Career of Hernando de Soto in the Conquest of Florida, as Told by a Knight of Elvas and in a Relation by Luys Hernandez de Biedma, Factor of the Expedition.* New York: Bradford Club. Reprinted, London: David Nutt, 1905; New York: Allerton Book Co., 1922; Gainesville: Palmetto Books, 1968. (20)

[174] Smith, Daniel M. 1960. "James Seagrove and the Mission to Tuckaubarchee, 1793." *Georgia Historical Quarterly* 44:41–55. (34)

[175]   Smoot, Joseph G., ed. 1965. "An Account of Alabama Indian Missions and Presbyterian Churches in 1828 from the Travel Diary of William S. Potts." *Alabama Review* 18:134–52.   (50)

[176]   Speck, Frank G. 1907. "The Creek Indians of Taskigi Town." *Memoirs of the American Anthropological Association* 2, part 2. Lancaster, Pa.: New Era Publishing Company. Reprinted, Millwood, N.Y.: Kraus, 1974.   (14)

[177]   ———. 1911. "Ceremonial Songs of the Creek and Yuchi Indians." Music transcr. Jacob D. Sapir. *University of Pennsylvania Museum Anthropological Publications* 1(2):157–245. Philadelphia: University Museum.   (14)

[178]   ———. 1947. "Notes on Social and Economic Conditions among the Creek Indians of Alabama in 1941." *America Indigena* 7:195–98.   (70)

[179]   ———. 1949. "The Road to Disappearance: Creek Indians Surviving in Alabama, a Mixed Culture Community." *American Anthropologist* 51:681–82.   (70)

[180]   Spoehr, Alexander. 1941. "Brief Communications: Creek Inter-Town Relations." *American Anthropologist* 43:132–33.   (11)

[181]   ———. 1947. "Changing Kinship Systems: A Study in the Acculturation of the Creeks, Cherokee, and Choctaw." *Field Museum of Natural History Anthropological Series* 33:153–235.   (11, 70)

[182]*   Stern, Theodore C. 1977. "The Creeks." In *The Native Americans: Ethnology and Backgrounds of the North American Indians,* ed. Robert F. Spencer, Jesse D. Jennings, et al., pp. 424–44. 2d ed. New York: Harper and Row.   (14)

[183]   Strickland, Rennard. Forthcoming. "The Five Civilized Tribes." In *Southeast,* ed. Raymond D. Fogelson. Vol. 14 of *The Handbook of North American Indians,* gen. ed. William C. Sturtevant. Washington, D.C.: Government Printing Office for the Institution. See [65].   (14)

[184]   Sturtevant, William C. 1971. "Creek into Seminole." In *North American Indians in Historical Perspective,* ed. Eleanor

Leacock and Nancy Oesterich Lurie,
pp. 92–128. New York: Random
House.   (viii)

[185]   ———. 1975. "Commentary." In
*Eighteenth-Century Florida and Its Border-
lands*, ed. Samuel Proctor, pp. 40–47.
Gainesville: University of Florida Press. (31)

[186]   ———, gen. ed. 1978–. *Handbook of
North American Indians*. 20 vols. Wash-
ington, D.C.: Government Printing
Office for the Smithsonian Institution.   (See
                                          [65])

[187]   Swan, Caleb. 1851–57. "Position and
State of Manners and Arts in the
Creek, or Muscogee Nation in 1791." In
*Historical and Statistical Information Re-
specting the History, Condition and Pros-
pects of the Indian Tribes of the United
States*, Henry Rowe Schoolcraft
5:251–83. See [171].   (33)

[188]   Swanton, John R. 1912. "The Creek
Indians as Mound Builders." *American
Anthropologist* 14:320–24.   (2)

[189] ———. 1917. "The Social Significance of the Creek Confederacy." *Proceedings of the International Congress of Americanists* 19:327–34. (8)

[190] ———. 1922. *Early History of the Creek Indians and Their Neighbors.* United States Bureau of American Ethnology Bulletin 73. Washington, D.C.: Government Printing Office. Reprinted, New York: Johnson, 1970. (17)

[191]* ———. 1922. "Tokulki of Tulsa." In *American Indian Life,* ed. Elsie Clews Parsons, pp. 127–45. New York: B. W. Huebsch. Reprinted, Lincoln: University of Nebraska Press, 1974. (13)

[192] ———. 1928. "Aboriginal Culture of the Southeast." In *Forty-second Annual Report of the United States Bureau of American Ethnology (1924–25),* pp. 673–726. Washington, D.C.: Government Printing Office. (6)

[193] ———. 1928. "Religious Beliefs and Medical Practices of the Creek Indians." In *Forty-second Annual Report of the*

United States Bureau of American Ethnology (1924–25), pp. 473–672. Washington, D.C.: Government Printing Office.   (13)

[194]*   ———. 1928. "Social Organization and Social Usages of the Indians of the Creek Confederacy." In *Forty-second Annual Report of the United States Bureau of American Ethnology (1924–25),* pp. 25–472. Washington, D.C.: Government Printing Office. Reprinted as a monogrpah, New York: Johnson, 1970. (9, 11, 13)

[195]   ———, ed. 1932. "The Green Corn Dance." *Chronicles of Oklahoma* 10:170–95.   (12)

[196]   ———. 1946. *The Indians of the Southeastern United States.* United States Bureau of American Ethnology Bulletin 137. Washington, D.C.: Government Printing Office. Reprinted, Grosse Pointe, Mich.: Scholarly Press, 1969; Washington, D.C.: Smithsonian Institution, 1978.   (21)

[197]   ———. 1932. "Ethnological Value of the DeSoto Narratives." *American Anthropologist* 34:570–90.   (20)

[198]   Tanner, Helen Hornbeck. 1975. "Pipesmoke and Muskets: Florida Indian Intrigues of the Revolutionary Era." In *Eighteenth-Century Florida and Its Borderlands,* ed. Samuel Proctor, pp. 13–39. Gainesville: University Presses of Florida.   (28)

[199]   Thomas, Daniel H. 1960. "Fort Toulouse: The French Outpost at the Alibamos on the Coosa." *Alabama Historical Quarterly* 22:141–230.   (26)

[200]   Trickett, Dean. 1940. "The Civil War in the Indian Territory." *Chronicles of Oklahoma* 17:315–27, 401–12; 18:142–53, 266–80.   (55)

[201]   Turner, Clarence W. 1932. "Events among the Muskogees during Sixty Years." *Chronicles of Oklahoma* 10:21–34.   (64)

[202]   Twiggs, Gen. John. 1927. "The Creek Troubles of 1793." *Georgia Historical Quarterly* 11:274–80.   (34)

[203]   Underhill, Lonnie E. 1971. "Hamlin Garland and the Final Council of the

Creek Nation." *Journal of the West* 10:511–20. (69)

[204]   Walker, Amelia. 1977. "Instant Indians: An Analysis of Cultural Identity in the American South." *Southern Anthropologist* 6:(2). (71)

[205]   Walker, Willard. Forthcoming. "The Creeks." In *Southeast,* ed. Ramond D. Fogelson. Vol. 14 of *Handbook of North American Indians,* gen. ed. William C. Sturtevant. Washington, D.C.: Government Printing Office for the Smithsonian Institution. See [65]. (14)

[206]   Waring, Antonio J. 1960. *Laws of the Creek Nation.* Athens: University of Georgia Libraries Miscellaneous Publications 1. (43)

[207]   Whitaker, Arthur P. 1928. "Alexander McGillivray, 1783–1793." *North Carolina Historical Quarterly* 5:181–203, 289–309. (29)

[208]   Willey, Gordon R., and William H.

Sears. 1952. "The Kasita Site." *Southern Indian Studies* 4:3–18. (3)

[209] Wilson, L. M. S. 1966. "Reminiscences of Jim Tomm." *Chronicles of Oklahoma* 44:290–306. (64)

[210] Woodward, Thomas S. 1859. *Woodward's Reminiscences of the Creek, or Muscogee Indians, Contained in Letters to Friends in Georgia and Alabama.* Montgomery, Ala.: Barrett and Wimbish. New ed., Tuscaloosa, Ala.: Alabama Book Store, 1929. Reprint of original in facsimile, Mobile, Ala.: Southern University Press, 1965; Atlanta: Georgia Department of Archives and History, 1974. (41)

[211] Wright, J. Leitch, Jr. 1967. "Creek-American Treaty of 1790: Alexander McGillivray and the Diplomacy of the Old Southwest." *Georgia Historical Quarterly* 51:379–400. (32)

[212] ———. 1967. *William Augustus Bowles, Director General of the Creek Nation.* Athens: University of Georgia Press. (33)

[213]   Wright, Muriel H. 1951. *A Guide to the Indian Tribes of Oklahoma*. Norman: University of Oklahoma Press. Reprinted, 1977.   (17, 70)

[214]   ———. 1957. "A Report to the General Council of the Indian Territory Meeting at Okmulgee in 1873." *Chronicles of Oklahoma* 34:7–16.   (59)

[215]   Young, Mary E. 1955. "The Creek Frauds: A Study in Conscience and Corruption." *Journal of American History* 42:411–37.   (45)

[216]   ———. 1961. *Redskins, Ruffleshirts and Rednecks: Indian Allotments in Alabama and Mississippi, 1830–1860*. Norman: University of Oklahoma Press.   (45)

The Newberry Library
Center for the History of the American Indian
Founding Director: D'Arcy McNickle
Director: Francis Jennings

Established in 1972 by the Newberry Library, in conjunction with the Committee on Institutional Cooperation of eleven midwestern universities, the Center makes the resources of one of America's foremost research libraries in the Humanities available to those interested in improving the quality and effectiveness of teaching American Indian history. The Newberry's collections include some 100,000 volumes on the history of the American Indian and offer specialized resources for studying historical aspects of Indian-White relations and Indian linguistics. The Center also assists Native Americans engaged in writing tribal histories and developing educational materials.

ADVISORY COMMITTEE

Chairman: Alfonso Ortiz
University of New Mexico

Robert F. Berkhofer
University of Michigan

Robert V. Dumont, Jr.
Native American Educational Services/Antioch College; Fort Peck Reservation

Raymond D. Fogelson
University of Chicago

William T. Hagan
State University of New York College, Fredonia

Nancy O. Lurie
Milwaukee Public Museum

Cheryl Metoyer-Duran
University of California, Los Angeles

N. Scott Momaday
Stanford University

Father Peter J. Powell
St. Augustine Indian Center

Father Paul Prucha, s.j.
Marquette University

Faith Smith
Native American Educational Services/Antioch College; Chicago

Sol Tax
University of Chicago

Robert K. Thomas
Wayne State University

Robert M. Utley
Advisory Council on Historical Preservation; Washington, D.C.

Antoinette McNickle Vogel
Gaithersburg, MD.

Dave Warren
Institute of American Indian Arts

Wilcomb E. Washburn
Smithsonian Institution

DATE DUE